JESUS CHRIST

JESUS CHRIST

Yves Congar, O.P.

Translated by
Luke O'Neill

HERDER AND HERDER

1966
HERDER AND HERDER NEW YORK
232 Madison Avenue, New York 10016

Original edition: *Jesus Christ,*
published by Les Editions du Cerf,
Paris, 1965.

Nihil obstat: Brendan Lawlor
                  Censor Deputatus
Imprimatur: † Robert F. Joyce
                  Bishop of Burlington
                  December 24, 1965

Library of Congress Catalog Card Number: 66–16946

CONTENTS

5

Its term is the realization of perfect monothesism, *179*. 3. The "economic" exercise (the earthly administration of the redemption) of His lordship by Christ includes a duality of domains, Church and world, a struggle (the resistance of the Powers and of the flesh), and, in Christ Himself, a priestly mode of suffering Servant, *183*.

ABBREVIATIONS

AAS	*Acta Apostolicae Sedis*
Denz.	Denzinger, *Enchiridion Symbolorum*
DTC	*Dictionnaire de Théologie Catholique*
JTS	*Journal of Theological Studies*
NRT	*Nouvelle Revue Théologique*
PG	*Patrologia Graeca* (Migne)
PL	*Patrologia Latina* (Migne)
RB	*Revue Biblique*
RechScRel	*Recherches de Science Religieuse*
TWNT	*Theologisches Wörterbuch zum Neuen Testament*

First Part

Christ
the Image of the Invisible God

Christ the Image of the Invisible God[1]

CHRIST the revealer of God. —The incarnation restores meaning to the world. —Divine transcendence and "philanthropy." —Towards a return to the living God. —Conclusions.

Christ the Revealer of God

The Christmas Preface, which has been attributed to St. Gregory the Great,[2] gives thanks to God "because by the mystery of the Word incarnate, a new light of your glory has shone upon the eyes of our mind; as we acknowledge Him to be God now visible, so may He draw us to the love of things invisible." It is of no particular importance that St. Gregory, in meditating upon the incarnate Word, is looking most of all for a moral pattern, for an invitation to turn towards the contemplation of heavenly things. What most interests us is, rather, the role of the Word incarnate as revealer of God, or, still more precisely, the value of the very fact of the incarnation to do just that.

The idea is a thoroughly biblical one. St. Paul, who did not know Christ according to the flesh, thinks of Him principally as the *substance* of the divine revelation which had been made to the Apostle. Still, he does not hesitate to apply to Christ the bib-

1 Appeared in *La Maison-Dieu*, no. 59 (third quarter, 1959), pp. 132–161.
2 B. CAPELLE, "La Préface de Noël," in *Questions Liturgiques et Paroissiales*, December, 1933, pp. 273–283; "La main de saint Grégoire dans le Sacramentaire grégorien," in *Revue Bénédictine*, 1937, pp. 13–28.

lical themes of the Wisdom books: *Christ is the image of the invisible God,* the splendor of His glory, and the stamp of God's very being.[3] An ancient hymn, quoted in the First Letter to Timothy, speaks of "the mystery of our religion . . . who was manifested in the flesh" (1 Tim 3:16). The synoptic Gospels present Jesus as a teacher, as the teacher of a justice other than the justice of the Pharisees, other even than the justice of the Law. At the time of His transfiguration, Jesus first appears with Moses and Elijah—the Law and the prophets—at His side; but when the apostles raise their eyes from the ground, to which they had cast themselves in awesome fear, they see only Jesus, as a voice calls from the clouds: "This is my beloved Son; listen to him." His right to be heard is based, then, on the fact that He is the Son of God, that He communicates the awareness which He possessed within the intimacy of the Father.

The whole of St. John's Gospel resounds with this idea. While the first three Gospels had told the story of the evangelical Word as it had unfolded from its beginning in the preaching of John the Baptist—"The beginning of the Gospel . . . John the baptizer appeared in the wilderness" (Mk 1:1f.), the fourth evangelist points out that this beginning is not only historical and earthly. The Word which rang out, nineteen centuries ago in Palestine, has its real beginning in the eternal Word: "In the beginning was the Word, and the Word was with God, and the Word was God." *This* is the eternal and divine Word which was made flesh and came to dwell among us. So true is this that what was really heard in His teaching was the teaching *of God.* "No one has ever seen God; the only Son, who is in the bosom of the Father, he has made him known" (Jn 1:19; cf. 6:46). To the Jews who asked: "How is it that a man untrained [in rabbinical studies] has such learning?", Jesus answered, "My teaching is not mine, but his who sent me" (Jn 7:15–16). And He claimed, again

[3] Cf. Col 1:15; Heb 1:3; compare 2 Cor 4:4, 6; 3:18; Rom 8:29 with Wis 7:25–26; Sir 24:3f.

and again, that He knew and that He was making known the one who had sent Him.[4]

God had long since spoken, and had thus made Himself known. But, in the events of sacred history and through the prophets, He had made Himself known as from afar; He had made Himself known only in His acts. Was He not to be heard, was He not to be seen—Himself? Even before the Greek soul had desired to see, and not merely to hear, Moses had been filled with that desire (Ex 33:18). There is no religious soul which does not desire to pass from shadows to Reality, from obedience to Presence.[5]

The whole thrust of the design of God was moving towards the perfection which is the communication of Himself. What is most proper to the new and eternal covenant lies precisely in the passage from the simple gifts of God to the gift of God himself, "from God who speaks to God made man."[6] St. Epiphanius quotes the following *agraphon* as coming from Christ: "He who spoke in the prophets is I, I who now stand before you."[7] It is in this sense that the liturgy for Christmas makes use of a phrase from Isaiah (52:6): *"Ego qui loquebar, ecce adsum"* (Vulgate). We find it again as the theme of the solemn prologue of the Letter to the Hebrews, to which we shall return: "In many and various ways God spoke of old to our fathers by the prophets; but in these last days he has spoken to us by a Son" (Heb 1:1–2).

[4] Cf. Jn 7:29; compare 12:49–50; 14:1–9.

[5] St. Bernard describes the just of the Old Testament as desiring to hear, no longer the prophets, but God Himself: *In Cant., Serm.* 7, 1–2 (PL 183, 789–790).

[6] This is the subtitle of the French edition of Louis BOUYER'S *The Meaning of Sacred Scripture,* Notre Dame, 1958. This difference between the two dispensations is brought out in Appendix III of our *The Mystery of the Temple,* Westminster, 1962; also in J. DE BACIOCCHI, "Présence eucharistique et transsubstantiation," in *Irénikon,* 32 (1959), pp. 139–160.

[7] A. RESCH, *Agrapha* (Texte und Untersuchungen, XXX, 3. 4.), Leipzig, 1906, p. 207.

15

When God is not content merely to speak through men, but constitutes Himself as the human word of revelation, there can be no question that He brings the final revelation. It was of an Other that the prophets had spoken, but in Jesus Christ it is *God Himself who speaks of Himself*. The first generations of Christians and the Fathers possessed, in a very vivid way, the joyous awareness of this great novelty: Jesus Christ has made us know God. Today, we are barely conscious of the value of this knowledge, brought to us by Christ. Religion strikes us as something which consists principally in the intentions and the sincerity of our hearts, or in good works. As far as we are concerned, salvation without any knowledge of God would be every bit as satisfactory. The Christians of antiquity were still surrounded by a paganism which had no knowledge of God, and no desire for it, and which even lacked the conviction that such knowledge was possible.[8] The Christians relished the joy and the confidence of having passed, thanks to Jesus Christ, from ignorance to knowledge of God, and they continually gave thanks for it. For them, Christ, the Word made man, was above all the revealer of God, the revealer of the Father who dwells in unapproachable light (1 Tim 6:16; cf. 1:7).[9] Indeed, as St. Leo frequently pointed out, God, invisible in His nature, became visible in ours.[10] Supreme revealer and completely true, Christ reveals, *ex parte* at least, the depth of the mystery of God and the First Truth.

But it is not God alone He reveals. He reveals also what it is to be in communion with Him, and the means and the joy of this communion. In 116–117, St. Ignatius of Antioch wrote to the

[8] Witness the scandal of Celsus in the face of the claims of the Christians; cf. M. HARL, *Origène et la fonction révélatrice du Verbe incarné* (Patristica Sorbonensia, 2), Paris, 1958, p. 76.

[9] This theme of ancient Christology, often neglected until recently, has been brought out in recent works, especially in M. HARL, *op. cit.,* p. 78, n. 27, with bibliographical material. See also the extracts at the end of this article.

[10] *Serm.* XXIII, 2 (*PL* 54, 201); *Epist.* 28 to Flavian, n. 4 (Denz., 144).

16

Ephesians: "Ignorance was dispelled, the former kingdom destroyed, when God appeared in the form of man *for a newness of eternal life.*"[11] A harmony exists among these three factors: the revealer, the truth revealed, the character of life or salvation, the means or the way of approaching this life. Jesus, who reveals the Father, also reveals the means; Jesus, who *is* the revealed truth of God, is also the way of approach: "Philip, he who sees me, sees the Father"; "I am the way" (Jn 14:9, 6). Jesus reveals the *heavenly* world, a world truly from above, and He reveals at the same time the paths of a life in communion with God, an other-than-earthly mode of existence: life according to the Spirit and the paths of Christian life.

This revelation is not contained in His teaching alone. It is also (and we should, perhaps, say *particularly*) in what He *did*. If we were to consider nothing but the teaching, we might see, in the humanity of Christ, little more than a mouth *for the Word,* who alone would be taken as the revealer of God. There is something of this approach in Origen, for example. Despite all his efforts to correct it, Origen never completely freed himself from the Alexandrian Platonism which sought everywhere the intelligible. Compared with the other comings of the Logos, all of them spiritual, the coming of the Word *in flesh* did not seem to him to occupy any privileged position. The flesh, after all, conceals more than it reveals.[12] And yet, the descent of the Word in our flesh, the assumption by God of the condition of a Servant,

[11] Eph 19:3. In the same perspective, St. Cyril of Alexandria emphasizes the sanctification *of the flesh* of Christ, for God's entry into this flesh is something far more than a simple metaphysical fact: it is ordered to the creation of a new man, to a renewal of human nature in the Spirit. Cf. his commentary on St. John and his *Sixth Dialogue on the Trinity* (PG 75, 1017); P. GALTIER, "Le Saint-Esprit dans l'Incarnation du Verbe d'après saint Cyrille d'Alexandrie," in *Problemi scelti di Teologia contemporanea,* Rome, 1954, pp. 383–392.

[12] See M. HARL, *op. cit.,* pp. 185, 201f., 205–218, 336–338.

the washing of the feet, the obedience in love even unto death on the cross, all have a value as revelation, and as revelation *of God:* "Philip, he who sees me, sees the Father."

The knowledge of God which has been brought by Christ is not a pure knowing. We see this already in the New Testament, but still more explicitly in the Fathers and in the early liturgies. This knowledge is both instruction and holiness. Not merely information preliminary to salvation, it is salvation already in act. St. Paul links the idea of being saved with the idea of coming to the knowledge of the truth (1 Tim 2:4). It is not without significance that baptism was so frequently called "enlightenment" or "faith" (Tertullian), but also "initiation." The fact is that saving knowledge has an importance which is not merely poetical, for it is the beginning, and therefore already the reality, of the communication of His own life and glory which God wishes to make to us. And yet, the descent of God to us is actually inseparable from our ascent to Him. Christ does not reveal the Father to us without attracting us to Him. The Word does not remain without effect (cf. Is 55:10–11). In the New Testament, the descent (*katabasis*) is bound up with an ascent (*anabasis, analepsis*); more precisely, God's descent to us is bound up with the progress of our ascent to God.[13] The Fathers understood this profoundly. It is, in fact, one of the reasons why it seemed to them that the redemption was won as soon as the incarnation occurred, that the Church was established as soon as God had come in our flesh. What has been referred to as the "physical theory" is, before all else, the expression of this extremely authentic and profound view of the mystery.

[13] See, among other texts, Jn 1:51; 3:13; 6:51, 62; Eph 4:8–10; Phil 2:7–11; Rom 1:17. A point which is strikingly expressed by St. FULGENTIUS, *Sermo in festo S. Stephani* (PL 65, 729–730), is that the fruit of the *descent* of Christ is the ascent of the saints, first celebrated the very next day after Christmas in the person of the first martyr.

The Incarnation Restores Meaning to the World

"A God made man for our salvation"

The Council of Chalcedon (451) fixed definitively the faith of the Church on the article of the incarnation: "true God and true man, consubstantial with the Father according to divinity and consubstantial with us according to humanity. . . ."[14] We would not be entering into the faith of the Church, as understood by the Fathers and by the New Testament, if we were to see in the incarnation a simple physical or, rather, metaphysical, fact, whose formula was given at Chalcedon: two natures, divine and human, united in the order of being in the one Person of the Son. . . . This is perfectly true, to be sure, but it is not in this alone that the mystery consists. Neither would it be sufficient to regard the metaphysical fact of the incarnation as the condition of an effective redemption, as something which would make possible the rendering to God of an infinite satisfaction and adoration. Such a view of the mystery would be more rich and less inadequate, but it would still be quite insufficient. Although it has the advantage over the former of putting the metaphysical fact of the incarnation in relation to the salvific design of God, it would nonetheless betray too dry, too unilinear, almost impoverished, a conception of this design.

The incarnation is essentially a fact, the most decisive fact in salvation history. This history is never lacking in ontological questions, but it cannot be reduced to them. Its mysteries can be understood only in relation to a design, by striving to grasp them as moments in an economy. From the theological point of view, the most interesting aspect of the programs of kerygmatic theology which have been outlined, from the years 1936–1939 on, by Fathers J. A. Jungmann and Hugo Rahner, seems to us to lie

[14] *Denz.,* 148.

19

in the effort they have made to see "*theo*-logy" once again in the framework of "economy."

In point of fact, God is not revealed in Himself, but is revealed to men, and as He wished to be *for them*. Consistently with this, there does not exist, either for the Fathers or for the apostolic writings, an incarnation in itself, isolated from what it is intended to be *for us: "propter nos et propter nostram salutem"* repeats the Council of Chalcedon, following the language of the councils of Nicaea and of Constantinople. Ignatius of Antioch viewed the entire economy or the divine plan as leading up "to the new man, Jesus Christ."[15] The orientation of the incarnation is towards the constitution of a new man whom we too must become, by inserting ourselves into Christ.[16] We know how unwearyingly the Fathers repeated: "The Son of God became man so that men might become God."[17] This means that the incarnation is what

15 Eph 20:1. And cf. *supra*, note 11.

16 Cf. St. HIPPOLYTUS, *De Antichristo*, 3 (Achelis edition, Leipzig, 1897, p. 6, 11. 17–19): "The Child of God is indeed unique, by whom even we have received the new birth of the Holy Spirit, so that our most profound aspiration here below is to be joined together, we who are many, with that unique heavenly man." In this extremely biblical perspective, the dual reading of Jn 1:13 takes on all its significance (*"nati sunt," "natus est"*).

17 Some examples: St. IRENAEUS, *Adversus Haereses*, III, 10, 2 (*PG* 7, 874); III, 19, 1 (939); IV, 44, 2 (1062A); V, preface (1120B); St. ATHANASIUS, *Orat. I contra Arianos*, 39; II, 70; III, 34 (*PG* 26, 92, 296, 397). *De Incarnatione Verbi*, 54 (*PG* 25, 192B); AMPHILOCHIUS OF ICONIUM, *Oratio in Christi Natalem*, 4 (*PG* 39, 41A); St. GREGORY OF NAZIANZEN, *Orat*. II, 22; XL, 45 (*PG* 35, 432 and 436, 424); St. GREGORY OF NYSSA, *Great Catechesis*, 27 (*PG* 45, 69); St. JOHN CHRYSOSTOM, *In Joan.*, 1, 14 (*PG* 59, 79); St. AMBROSE, *In Luc.*, book V, n. 46 (*PL* 15, 1648); St. AUGUSTINE, *Serm.* 125, 5; 127, 6, 9; 166, 4; 184, c. 3; 186, 2; 192, 1; 194, 3 (*PL* 38, 680, 710, 909, 997, 999, 1012, 1016); *Epist.* 140, 4, 10 (*PL* 32, 541f.); 187, 20 (*PL* 33, 839–840); *Enarr. in Ps.* 34, 21 (*PL* 36, 507); *De Civit. Dei*, IX, 15, 2; XXI, 15 (*PL* 41, 269, 729); AUGUSTINE [?], *Serm.* 128, 1 (*PL* 39, 1997, cited by St. THOMAS AQUINAS, IIIa, q. 1, a. 2); St. FULGENTIUS, *De Incarnatione* (Maxima Bibliotheca Veterum Patrum, Lyons, 1677, IX, 310); St. LEO, Serm. XXIII, 4; XXV, 2 (*PL* 54, 202, 209); THEOPHYLACT, *Enarr. in Ev. Joan.*, c. 1 (*PG* 123, 1156). See also the studies of J. GROSS, M. LOT-BORODINE on divinization in the Greek Fathers; A. SPINDELER, *Cur Verbum caro factum? Das Motiv der Menschwerdung und das Verhältnis der Erlösung zur Mensch-*

God willed that it be, and is what He made it, only if we keep in mind the link which it possesses or intends to effect with creation as a whole, and most particularly with man, who is creation's summing-up and point (microcosm).

From one standpoint, the incarnation is connected to the world, whose meaning it restores (we do not intend to put any more emphasis on this point, despite its importance). From another standpoint, the incarnation is connected to the entire salvific activity of Christ. This was understood remarkably well by St. Thomas Aquinas, who introduced the Third Part of his *Summa* with these words: "Our Saviour and Lord Jesus Christ, 'in delivering His people from their sins,' as the Angel announced, revealed Himself to us as the way of truth by which we have been made capable of coming to resurrection and to the blessedness of immortal life."[18] In a single treatise, St. Thomas studies first the mystery of the incarnation in itself, "the mystery of God made man for our salvation," and then the *acta et passa* of the incarnate God, namely, the entire redemptive activity of Christ, achieved in the life and the Pasch of the Saviour. If the mystery of the incarnation is one of "a God made man for our salvation," we cannot separate from it anything in which His redemptive intention was accomplished. The *acta et passa Christi in carne* are part of this mystery. The Fathers, we think, would have subscribed to the words of Péguy: the agony, the death of Jesus, His cry, *Eli, Eli. . .* , all of this is the completion of the incarnation, for in all of this God constitutes Himself "true man" (first *Clio*). But we can very well add that if the incarnate Word is the revealer of God, His *acta et passa* also possess the value of a revelation of God.

---

werdung Gottes in den christologischen Glaubenskämpfen des 4. u. 5. Jahr., Paderborn, 1938; J. LOOSEN, *Logos und Pneuma im begnadeten Menschen nach Maximus Confessor,* Münster, 1941; K. BORNHÄUSER, *Die Vergottungslehre des Athanasius u. Joh. Damascenus,* 1903.

[18] St. THOMAS AQUINAS, *Summa Theologiae,* IIIa, Prologue.

In the perspective of Scripture, the liturgy, and the Fathers, the nativity itself involves the continuation of the mysteries of salvation, whose culmination is the Pasch.

St. Paul does not view the Lord's coming in the flesh other than in the line of the Pasch: sacrifice (Phil 2:7–8; Heb 10:5–7), resurrection (Rom 1:3–4) and glory (Phil 2:7–11), redemption (Gal 2:4–5). What is more, since Christ's existence according to the flesh holds no special interest for him (2 Cor 5:16), the Apostle sees the divine Sonship of the Lord declaring itself in His resurrection, followed by His being seated at the right hand of the Father.[19]

Not long ago, J. Pinsk[20] demonstrated very effectively that the Roman liturgy for Christmas does not separate the celebration of the historical fact, or remembrance, which is so striking in this feast, from the whole mystery of the redemption, the whole plan of salvation, whose purpose is the divinization of man, nor, indeed, from the mystery of God Himself. The distribution of resonances of the three births—eternal, historical, spiritual—over the three Masses of Christmas, such as St. Thomas proposes,[21] has about it a rather artificial air. But St. Thomas was not under any illusions about this, as can be seen from what follows in his text. The truth is that the liturgy does in fact unite, in a single memorial, the transcendent principle, its sacrament in history, and its definitive fruit; in short, the triple and interdependent reality of our sonship in grace, the temporal birth of Christ, and His eternal generation.[22] What Christmas aims at is our divinization, hence our redemption by the Pasch of the Lord. These can

[19] Cf. Acts 13:32–33; Rom. 1:4; compare 8:11; Heb 1:5; 5:5.
[20] "La venue du Seigneur dans la liturgie de Noël," in *Questions Liturgiques et Paroissiales,* December, 1933, pp. 259–272.
[21] IIIa, q. 88, a. 2, ad 2.
[22] Compare E. FLICOTEAUX, "Le mystère de Noël," in *La Vie Spirituelle,* 7 (December, 1922), pp. 282–304. The liturgy celebrates only the heavenly births and those earthly births which are immediately related to the incarnation: that of John the Baptist and that of the Mother of God.

22

be realized *because* He who was born, died, rose, and ascended to heaven is no other than the Son of God. The whole is a single mystery of covenant, just as the *"admirabile commercium"* of the incarnation is totally ordered to that of the ascension and that of Pentecost, which are the terms of a Pasch, a "passover" whose beginning is the cross.[23] There is seemingly no end of texts in the Christmas liturgy which speak of redemption.[24]

The Eastern liturgy expresses the same understanding of the mystery. Christmas is announced in the liturgical calendars in this fashion: "Pasch, holy day of three days' duration."[25] Although the triodia and canons of the vigil might very well be the work of Simeon Metaphrastes (eleventh century), they express an understanding of the feast for which a great number of ancient witnesses, patristic and liturgical, can be found. It is an understand-

[23] See P. MIQUEL, "Le mystère de l'Ascension," in *Questions Liturgiques et Paroissiales,* June, 1959, pp. 105–126, especially pp. 122f. The author, who quotes the orations of the feast of the ascension (Leonine), could have compared as well the oration *super oblata* from the Midnight Mass: *"Ut tua gratia largiente, per haec sacrosancta commercia in illius inveniamur forma, in quo tecum est nostra substantia"* (FELTOE edition, Cambridge, 1896, p. 161; MOHLBERG edition, Münster, 1927, n. 1249).

[24] E. FLICOTEAUX has pointed them out. One of the most striking is the *De Profundis* of Vespers. See *art. cit.* St. LEO calls Christmas *"salutis nostrae sacramentum"* (*Serm.* XXII, 1), *"sacramentum humanae restitutionis"* (*Serm.* XXV, 1). The liturgy, in the West as well as in the East, is filled with the idea that the incarnation (Christmas) is the beginning of the redemptive restoration: cf. G. B. LADNER, *The Idea of Reform. Its Impact on Christian Thought and Action in the Age of the Fathers,* Cambridge (Mass.), 1959, pp. 284f.; E. WEIGL, "Die Oration 'Gratiam tuam, quaesumus, Domine.' Zur Geschichte des 25 März in der Liturgie," in *Passauer Studien,* 1953, pp. 57–73 (our prayer of the Angelus). The comparison of the crib with an altar occurs frequently in the Greek Fathers (St. John Chrysostom, Theodotus of Ancyra, etc.). It was often taken over and translated into plastic terms in the medieval iconography of the West: E. MALE, *L'art religieux du XIIe siècle en France,* 6ᵉ édition, Paris, 1953, ch. III; *L'art religieux du XIIIe siècle en France,* 7ᵉ édition, Paris, 1931, pp. 185f. In her lovely poem, *L'attente de Jésus,* Marie Noël has shown the cross being somehow superimposed, point by point, on Mary's preparation of her baby's outfit.

[25] See Th. SPASSKIJ, "La Pâque de Noël," in *Irénikon,* 30 (1957), pp. 289–306. We are only indirectly acquainted with K. ONASCH, *Das Weihnachtsfest im Orthodoxen Kirchenjahr. Liturgie u. Ikonographie,* Berlin, Evang. Verlagsanstalt, 1958.

ing which is extremely profound. Christmas, that is, the incarnation, is the beginning of the kenosis or abasement of God in the condition of Servant. This is wholly in line with the meaning of the hymn quoted by St. Paul in the Letter to the Philippians (2:7–11). Let us quote a few of these patristic and liturgical texts.

"The Word of God, incorporeal, immortal, and simple, came into our world. Not that He had ever been far from it before— for He was absent from no part of creation; coexistent with the Father, He filled all in all (cf. Eph 1:23; Col 3:11)—but He came, He descended, out of kindness towards us and to reveal Himself to us."[26]

"Our Lord Jesus Christ, His only-begotten Son. . . , who, in these last times, for our salvation, took the form of a slave and became man, dwelt with human nature, was crucified, and rose again on the third day."[27]

"He for whom being equal to God is no robbery shows Himself to us in the form of a servant."[28]

"The unchanged image of the Father takes the form of a servant."[29]

The anaphora of the liturgy of St. Basil also evokes Philippians 2:6 before citing Romans 5:12. We find the same approach in the liturgy of St. Gregory Nazianzen, in Theodore of Mopsuestia in his catechetical homilies and anaphora, etc.[30] This process of

[26] St. ATHANASIUS, cited by J. SUICER, *Thesaurus ecclesiasticus, e patribus graecis ordine alphabetico exhibens,* Amsterdam, 1682, under συγκατὰβασις.

[27] St. JOHN CHRYSOSTOM, *Huit Catéchèses baptismales inédites,* edited by A. WENGER (Sources chrétiennes, 50, Paris, 1957, p. 119) : Cat. 1, 21.

[28] Introduction of the first troparion inserted in the canon on December 20th, a feast in anticipation of Christmas.

[29] Stichera of Christmas Vespers, eighth century (quoted by SPASSKIJ, *art. cit.*).

[30] The texts are cited in L. LIGIER, "Autour du sacrifice eucharistique. Anaphores orientales et Anamnèse juive de Kippur," in *NRT,* 82 (1960), pp. 40–55 (pp. 49–50).

24

relating the incarnation to the program of salvation through the recapitulation in Christ, the Second Adam, of the destiny of death of the first Adam, is a basic theme in the liturgical and dogmatic tradition of the Church. In the Fathers, this moment of Christmas, as already paschal, is brought out in various ways. First, in the soteriological argument, so frequently used in the Trinitarian and Christological disputes of the fourth and fifth centuries, although it had been made even before then, since we find it formally in St. Irenaeus and germinally in St. Ignatius of Antioch.[31] The Alexandrian Fathers, Athanasius and Cyril, the Cappadocians, and Tertullian, Ambrose and Augustine as well, never tire of arguing thus: Nothing in man has been saved but that which was assumed by the Son of God in His incarnation; our own resurrection, the supreme article of Christian faith and hope, is assured only if the resurrection of Christ is real, only if God *really* became man.

The idea of connecting our birth according to grace with the birth of Christ according to the flesh seems to have been most particularly dear to St. Leo, as well as to St. Maximus (or the author who has been published under his name).[32] A mind nourished on St. Paul might well be surprised at first to see our *heavenly* birth *according to the Spirit* linked to the birth of Christ *according to the flesh*. He who gives us life is, in fact, not Christ inasmuch as He is conformed to the first Adam, "born of woman, born under the law" (Gal 4:4: the only reference in St. Paul to the Virgin Mary), precisely because *He died* under this aspect. Christ became "life-giving spirit," principle of justification and of new life, heavenly life, only by a resurrection accord-

---

31 IGNATIUS, *Smyrn.*, 4, 2; IRENAEUS, *Adversus Haereses*, V, 1, 1–3 (*PG* 7, 1121f.); *Epideixis*, 39 (*Patrologia Orientalis*, XII, 775). See E. MERSCH, *The Whole Christ*, Milwaukee, 1938, Index, p. 600, under "Argument: D. The Soteriological Argument."
32 St. LEO THE GREAT, *Sermo* XXVI, 2; XXIX, 3; St. MAXIMUS, *Hom.* XV (*PL* 57, 254); PSEUDO-MAXIMUS, *Hom.* IX (*PL* 57, 245).

ing to the Spirit.[33] This may be a point of New Testament teaching which could be more carefully studied by those who think it possible to establish a spiritual maternity of the Virgin Mary, in regard to the Mystical Body, directly on her character as Mother of God according to the flesh. St. Leo does not make this application, and proceeds in precise fashion. He links the spiritual and, ultimately, heavenly birth of Christians, or the complete creation of the New Man, with the temporal birth of the Word and also with the eternal birth as only-begotten Son, by way of the Pasch of Christ and the baptism of Christians, which bring the births together at that Pasch, and not at Christmas.[34] By bringing the entire saving process into his line of vision, from abasement up to death, and from exaltation up to heaven, in short, the entire Pasch of Christ crowning His condition of servant, Christmas is seen, in all truth, as the mystery of "a God made man for our salvation" (St. Thomas, *Summa,* IIIa, Prologue).

This salvific activity is, from first to last, condescension (*sunkatabasis*), kenosis, filial obedience, and service in love. It is the "recapitulation," as St. Irenaeus used the word, of the Fall. It is, that is to say, the reprise (though in the opposite sense) of all

[33] See, generally, the Letter to the Galatians; Rom 1:3–4 (and the commentary of St. AUGUSTINE, *Ep. ad Rom. inchoata Expos.,* 5, PL 35, 2091; *De praedestinatione sanctorum,* 15, PL 44, 982–983); Rom 4:25; 6:1–11; 8:1–13; 1 Cor 15:20–23, 45–50; 2 Cor 5:16–21; 13:4; 1 Tim 3:16; 2 Tim 2:8; compare 1 Pet 3:18.

[34] See *Sermo* XXVI, 2 (*PL* 54, 213): "Today's feast renews for us the sacred coming of Jesus, born of the Virgin Mary. It is in adoring the nativity of our Saviour that we celebrate our own origins. The birth of Christ is indeed the beginning of the Christian people, and the anniversary day of the head is also that of the body. If each in his turn is called, if all the sons of the Church are spread over the succeeding ages, still the totality of the faithful, come forth from the baptismal fonts, crucified with Christ in His passion, risen in His resurrection, placed in His ascension at the right hand of the Father, are born today with Him. . . ." Compare *Serm.* XXI, 3; XXV, 5; *Epist.* 16 ad episc. Siciliae, *"nisi proprie voluisset intelligi regenerationis gratiam ex sua resurrectione coepisse"* (PL 54, 699). On the rapports between incarnation and redemption according to St. Leo, see Appendix I of M. B. DE SOOS, *Le mystère liturgique d'après saint Léon,* Münster, 1958.

the historical factors through which man was lost and continued to endorse his loss. By desiring to exalt himself, man had degraded himself and had fallen. By agreeing to descend, man is once more, in Christ, set on his feet and once more takes up the path of glory.

Before going any further, we would like to put some emphasis on two significant points. They are consequences or applications of this way, faithful both to the New Testament and to tradition, of approaching the incarnation as something inseparable from the whole of salvific activity and from the goal at which it aims, the salvation or divinization of man.

1. First of all, in theology *de Ecclesia*. We are aware of the extent to which the mystery of the Church imitates the mystery of the incarnate Word. We see too that it must find an analogous equilibrium, through a kind of ecclesiological Chalcedon.[35] The Christological theme which we have just been developing can inspire a new parallel, whose full importance will be grasped by those who follow ideological currents in this era of ecumenism. We must not, in the case of the Church, any more than in the case of Christ, separate ontology from mission, or—if I might speak in such fashion—the morphology from the physiology, and even from the function or external activity. We can no more reduce the mystery of the incarnation to a pure metaphysical fact, no more reduce it to its ontological formula, than we can conceive of the mystery of the Church, and even of her unity, merely on a static plane, like some organizational or institutional fact. For their aim and their ambit are the missionary activity of the communication of salvation. When we speak of the Church, and of her unity as well, we must never lose sight of the fact that she is not made for herself, but for apostolic service to the world.

[35] See our *Christ, Our Lady, and the Church,* Westminster, 1957; "Dogme christologique et Ecclésiologie. Vérité et limites d'un parallèle," in *Sainte Eglise* (Unam Sanctam, 41), Paris, 1963, pp. 69–104.

2. Secondly, in the theology of created or earthly realities. Neither are we able to separate this theology, so closely connected with that of the incarnate Word, from the plan of God, which is Christological and paschal.[36] The truth is that we must avoid the tendency to remain on the level of abstract and formal analysis. Although this is a legitimate, and even necessary, stage of reflection, we must, if we want to speak of realities as they *are,* see them in the light of their concrete existential conditions. What we encounter, then, is a world foreseen, from the very beginning, as sinful and as redeemed *in Christo* and *ad Christum.*[37] In the eternal plan of God, the Word is conceived as *incarnandus.* . . . We have had the experience ourselves: how great an effort is demanded of a mind formed in the school of St. Thomas to give full honor to these truths! But we can no more stop at a purely formal ontological consideration of things than we can be satisfied by a metaphysics of the hypostatic union. A complete theology of earthly realities cannot be a pure theology of incarnation. It must, in the final analysis, be Christological, paschal, eschatological.

Divine Transcendence and "Philanthropy"

"Who is, who was, who is to come"

"In many and various ways God spoke of old to our fathers by the prophets; but in these last days he has spoken to us by a Son, whom he appointed the heir of all things, through whom also he created the world" (Heb 1:1–2). This text is read as the epistle for the day Mass on Christmas. Between the two moments of manifestation of God which it distinguishes, both continuity

[36] See W. KUNNETH, *Theologie der Auferstehung,* Munich, 1951, and the critique of Chanoine G. Thils's study by D. V. WARNACH, in *Theologische Revue,* 1952, col. 172.
[37] Cf. Eph 1:14, Col 1:16–17; Heb 1:3; 1 Cor 8:6.

and opposition exist. We would do well to support our meditation by an image, as well-sustained and as concrete as possible, of the framework of the manifestations and of the substance put forward in each of these two moments: the prophets and the Son.

The long procession of prophets from Moses to John the Baptist! Thirteen or fifteen centuries of advances by God. There is Moses, the Moses of Michelangelo, of the well at the Charterhouse of Champol, now to be seen at the Dijon Museum. Better still, the Moses of the biblical texts, the man who faces up to Pharaoh, the man who, supported by faith in God's promise, alone brings a stubborn and sensual people through forty years in the desert. Moses, the man of Sinai, who met God and spoke to Him, mouth-to-mouth as it were, in a landscape which even today is chaotic, sun-scorched, harshly majestic and solitary. . . . Or Isaiah, again the prophet as we see him today at the museum in Dijon, or the one of the portal at Chartres: a seer. He beheld Yahweh of battles in royal majesty, in the sacred precincts of the Temple (cf. Is 6:1–4, quoted below). What greatness among these prophets! What men they were, what giants! In them, all was strength, intransigence, boldness, austerity. . . .

When, after the prophets themselves and the setting of their visions, we consider their message, we find, as the dominant element, the affirmation of the absolute character of the reign of God: Yahweh is King, He alone is Lord. Certain demands, formidable consequences come with this affirmation. The remarkable thing is that the suddenness and even, occasionally, awfulness of this reign is somehow tempered, or rather completed, by a note of tenderness, familiarity, mercy. We read that the Messiah will rule the nations like a conquering warrior, with an iron rod,[38] but also that he will be "the good shepherd," watching carefully over his flock with unsparing care (Ez 34; Jer 23:1–8). We hear of the Messiah as a new David, called to

[38] Ps 2:9; compare Deut 28:48; Jer 28:13–14; but also Rev 2:27; 12:5; 19:15.

29

reign,[39] but we hear of him also as a meek and suffering servant who takes upon himself and bears the evil of all, that he might reconcile all.[40] "Yahweh is a devouring fire, a jealous God" (Deut 4:24), and yet He feels for His people a love which is somehow inextinguishable, unrepentant, a love whose tenderness and inexhaustible capacity for forgiveness are revealed to us in the shattering tale of Hosea and his "wife of fornication"— surely one of the supreme moments of the revelation of God in the Old Testament.

The prophet is a man who makes Justice descend upon the earth, as Léon Bloy put it. Justice, and the fire of heaven! But now it is God Himself who speaks, God who makes Himself known, no longer now from afar, and through the mouths of other men, held fast by His powerful hands. It is God Himself, in person. "*Ego qui loquebar, ecce adsum.*" We sit up and take notice: what shall we hear? We draw near: what shall we see? Now, when God Himself begins to speak, when He shows Himself in person, when He unveils His hidden depths, when the Invisible is made visible, what appears is "His goodness and loving kindness for men. *Apparuit benignitas et humanitas Salvatoris nostri Dei.*"[41] When God shows Himself to us in person, it is a man who appears, and even, at first, a tiny child.

The word "*philanthropia,*" used by St. Paul, has its origin in a pagan tongue, and is not found elsewhere in the New Testament. Once Christianity had assumed Hellenic culture (a task which was part of the mission and grace of the Fathers), this expression, which signified a sovereign's benevolence or generosity, shaded by mercy and kindness, became the tender philanthropy of God and a key word in the first stages of catechesis. The Fathers were fond of developing first the theme of the superabundant blessings of God and His love for men, as revealed in

39 Cf. 2 Sam 7; Ps 89; Is 9:6; Dan 7:14; Lk 1:32.
40 Is 42:1–3; 50:4–9; 52:13 to 53:12.
41 Tit 3:4; Epistle for the Dawn Mass.

creation, then in the way He dealt with man and, rather than letting him be lost, came down to help him and to save him.[42] The Eastern anaphoras, that of St. Serapion, for example, delight in calling upon God under the lovely name of "Friend of men."

Assuredly, God, if He is to reveal Himself to men who are involved in bodily life and in historical time, must take *another form* than His "*forma Dei.*" He can unveil Himself only in veiling Himself, can reveal Himself only in a kind of disguise. It is in the veil that He unveils Himself to eyes still earthly. This dialectic is the very condition of revelation. And yet, its paradoxical character must not lead us to forget that the reality and positive value of the revelation are linked to the form which it assumes, to the veil under which this revelation takes place.

The truth of the matter is that the wisdom of God, the closer it came to men, became all the more human.[43] God not only

[42] St. ATHANASIUS, *De Incarnatione Verbi*, 16 (*PG* 25, 124D–125A); St. JOHN CHRYSOSTOM, *Huit Catéchèses baptismales inédites*, edited by A. WENGER (Sources chrétiennes, 50, Paris, 1954), Cat. I, 3 (p. 110); I, 8 (p. 112); II, 1 (p. 134). Père Wenger quotes the beginning of an unpublished homily for Holy Thursday by Severien of Gabala: "The mercy and the goodness of God [*philanthropia*] burst forth in all creation, but especially in the mystery of the economy. . . ." See J. LECUYER, "Théologie de l'initiation chrétienne d'après les Pères," in *La Maison-Dieu*, no. 58, 1959, pp. 5–26. For the first four centuries, see H. PÉTRÉ, *Caritas. Etude sur le vocabulaire latin de la charité chrétienne*, Louvain, 1948, pp. 200–221. G. DOWNEY, "Philanthropia in Religion and Statecraft in the IVth Century after Christ," in *Historia*, 4 (1955), pp. 199–208 (many references to the Greek Fathers, pp. 204f., and to the Eastern liturgies, pp. 205–207). R. LE DEAUT, "Philanthrôpia dans la littérature grecque jusqu'au N.T.," in *Mélanges Eugène Tisserant*, I (Studi e Testi, 235), Rome, Vatican, 1964, pp. 255–294. For the subsequent development in the East, see J. SCHWEIGL, "Der Kult des *Philanthrôpos Sôter*, vom 1.–15. Jahrh.," in *Gregorianum*, 22 (1941), pp. 497–502. It was under this title that the feast of the Sacred Heart was introduced in the 1942 Roman edition of the *Liturgicon;* cf. J. SCHWEIGL, "De cultu liturgico 'Dulcissimi Domini et Dei et Salvatoris nostri Jesu Christi, Amatoris hominum' in ritu byzantino," in *Gregorianum*, 23 (1942), pp. 255–265.

[43] Compare Bar 3:36: ". . . he gave her to Jacob his servant and to Israel whom he loved. Afterwards she appeared on earth and lived among men" (text quoted by St. JOHN CHRYSOSTOM to show that the human coming of God had been foretold: *Quod Christus sit Deus*, n. 2, *PG* 48, 815. Compare Sir 24:8f.; Prov 8:31; Wis 9:10f.; and, finally, Jn 1:14.

speaks the language of man—He could not otherwise make Himself understood by men—but He shows Himself as human. We do not have here in mind merely those instances in which the Lord appeared in human form to the great heroes of the faith under the old dispensation: to Abraham, under the oak at Mambre (Gen 17), to Joshua (Josh 8:13–15), to Daniel (Dan 7).[44] We are thinking every bit as much about the profound significance, indicated by many exegetes,[45] of the constant anthropomorphisms of the Bible. God is again and again shown as having senses, as engaged in activities, as having feelings, which are analogous to the senses, activities, and feelings of men. Images such as these served to divert minds from a naturistic representation of God, but they also had a positive aim and content: they are connected with the development of the revelation of God as a *moral* God. Basically, their use was made legitimate by the fact that God had made man in His image and likeness (Gen 1:26). This fact, whose consequences are so extensive, is at the base of the very possibility of a relationship between the living God and man. If He speaks to us, if He communicates His Spirit to us, the reason is that there is, between Him and us, a fundamental kinship. "We are indeed his offspring," as St. Paul, quoting Aratus, says (Acts 17:28). Hence, there is in God, realized divinely, a kind of superior humanity.

[44] This fact was pointed out by EUSEBIUS (*Hist. Eccles.*, I, 2, 7; 11–12; 24–25) and, as regards Abraham, by almost all the Fathers (for the Ante-Nicene Fathers, cf. references in Bardy's edition of Eusebius, Sources chrétiennes, 31, 1952, p. 7).

[45] See, among others, J. BONSIRVEN, *Le Judaïsme palestinien au temps de Jésus-Christ*, Paris, 1935, t. I, pp. 145f., 221 (ET of the 1950 abridgment, *Palestinian Judaism in the Time of Jesus Christ*, New York, 1964, pp. 5–7); J. PEDERSEN, *Israel. Its Life and Culture*, London, 1940, vols. III–IV, pp. 647f.; T. BOMAN, *Hebrew Thought Compared with Greek*, Philadelphia, 1960, pp. 101f.; F. MICHAELI, *Dieu à l'image de l'homme*, Neuchâtel-Paris, 1950; L. BOUYER, *The Meaning of Sacred Scripture*, Notre Dame, 1958, p. 151; M. T. L. PENIDO, on the other hand, approaches the question in purely Greek, purely logical fashion, *Le rôle de l'Analogie en Théologie dogmatique* (Bibl. Thomiste, 15), Paris, 1931, pp. 81, 100.

Of course, we no sooner say this than we have to deny it. "Superior humanity" suggests the idea of a nature and of qualities which are the same but are simply transposed to a very high degree, while "realized divinely" signifies a distance which is positively immeasurable, a radical and irremediable disparity. God is God: between Him and us there is no distance which is positively immeasurable, no radical and irremediable disparity. God is God: between him and us, there is no common reality so all-embracing as to include both terms at once. "For my thoughts are not your thoughts, neither are your ways my ways. For as the heavens are higher than the earth, so are my ways higher than your ways and my thoughts than your thoughts" (Is 55:8–9). And even more besides! For there is, after all, some proportion between the heavens and the earth—we can calculate the celestial distances, we can gauge the temperature of the sun. . . —but, between God and us there is no such proportion. God is God!

And yet, what we say about Him, based on what He has first communicated to us, corresponds to a reality. We properly say, "based on what He has communicated to us." Without His word, we would never have dared to say, for example, that there is in Him a generation, a birth, a paternity, and a filiation. For these are human characteristics. . . . But the Church has taken pains to understand the statements of the New Testament in such a way as to preserve all their force, while respecting the transcendence and mystery of the sublime way in which they are verified in God. With the aid of the kind of dialectical knowledge studied in philosophy or theology under the heading of analogy, we are going to say what follows. What we want to grasp is the element of "*theo*-logy," that is to say, the element of revelation about *God*, which is contained in the event of Christmas, an event which is preëminently a feast of "the economy."

This *theo*-logy is expressed in a familiar formula. The most surprising thing, though, is not that Jesus Christ is God, but that *God is Jesus Christ.* There must, then, be in Him something which makes this possible, something beyond His omnipotence alone, which, of itself, is nothing but infinite possibility; something beyond the freedom of grace, which permits Him, who is so high, to stoop so low;[46] something there must be, and something positive, which led Him to be so condescending and to become man.

All through the Bible, God shows Himself both as transcendent and as bestowed, as very high and as very near. Absolute and perfect, He exists in His order of holiness, but He is wholly bent over towards us, wholly concerned with communicating Himself. It is remarkable indeed that these two aspects of biblical revelation, aspects which are apparently antinomical, not only coexist but are asserted in just those texts or just those episodes which must ultimately find their full truth in Jesus Christ. The effect of this is to show that transcendence, when it is the transcendence of the God of faith, cannot proceed without the condescension and familiarity of this very God, and reciprocally. Let us recall just three passages from the Old Testament:

1. "Jacob left Beer-sheba, and went toward Haran. And he came to a certain place, and stayed there that night, because the sun had set. Taking one of the stones of the place, he put it under his head and lay down in that place to sleep. And he

---

[46] Compare this fine passage from Barth who, having so powerfully championed the transcendence of God, discovers His "humanity": "How could God's deity exclude His humanity, since it is God's freedom for love and thus His capacity to be not only in the heights but also in the depths, not only great but also small, not only in and for Himself but also with another distinct from Him, and to offer Himself to him?" K. BARTH, *The Humanity of God,* Richmond (Va.), 1960, p. 49. St. BONAVENTURE made this profound observation: "*Hoc est maximum miraculum, ut quod Deus sit homo, primus sit novissimus* . . ." (*In Hexaemeron,* Col. III, 13, *Opera,* ed. Quaracchi, vol. V, p. 345b).

dreamed that there was a ladder set up on the earth, and the top of it reached to heaven; and behold, the angels of God were ascending and descending on it! And behold, the Lord stood above it [or: beside him] and said, 'I am the Lord, the God of Abraham your father. . . .' Then Jacob woke from his sleep and said, 'Surely the Lord is in this place, and I did not know it.' And he was afraid, and said, 'How awesome is this place! This is none other than the house of God, and this is the gate of heaven' " (Gen 28:10–13, 16–17).

Terribilis est locus iste! The liturgy repeats this cry in the Introit of the Mass of the Dedication of a Church. The presence of God arouses this religious fear which stems from the sense of His absolute holiness. Those who have experienced it close-at-hand feel it as something exceedingly great, exceedingly exalted![47] Jacob is awed; the place where God has touched the earth is awesome. But, at the same time, it is the place where *He touches* the earth, it is a place of communication, hence of nearness, a place of perpetual coming and going, from above to below, and from below above. Jesus applies this verse to Himself (Jn 1:51) to indicate His own body as the place, the only place, where God has truly touched the earth, the sole point at which is effected this coming and going of grace and of thanksgiving, of prayer and of bestowal.

2. "In the year that King Uzziah died I saw the Lord sitting upon a throne, high and lifted up; and his train filled the temple. Above him stood the seraphim; each had six wings: with two he

[47] It is unnecessary to have recourse to the analysis made by Rudolf Otto and historians of religion, of the union, in the "holy," of the *tremendum* and the *fascinosum.* We need only look to the experience of the saints. St. John, at the Last Supper, was leaning on Jesus's breast; yet, when he saw Him in the appearance recorded in the Book of Revelation, he fell at His feet, as though dead (Rev 1:17). St. Francis of Assisi, who was the first to make a *crèche,* at Greccio, can say no more on Alvernia than: "Who are you, O Lord, and who am I?"

covered his face, and with two he covered his feet, and with two he flew. And one called to another and said: 'Holy, holy, holy is the Lord of hosts; the whole earth is full of his glory.' And the foundations of the thresholds shook at the voice of him who called, and the house was filled with smoke. And I said: 'Woe is me! For I am lost; for I am a man of unclean lips, and I dwell in the midst of a people of unclean lips; for my eyes have seen the King, the Lord of hosts!'" (Is 6:1–5).

Isaiah saw the majesty of God, and he too took fright. How can one confront the presence of the thrice-Holy and not die? But the passage continues: "Then flew one of the seraphim to me, having in his hand a burning coal which he had taken with tongs from the altar. And he touched my mouth, and said: 'Behold, this has touched your lips; your guilt is taken away, and your sin forgiven.'" (vv. 7–8). The holiness, the purity of God, which keep Him separated and very far away, are communicated to the prophet; they will later be communicated to the people for whom the prophet is sent, in the obedience of faith, so that "the Holy One" will have a name which is somehow proper to Isaiah, "the Holy One *of Israel*." Nearness and communication accompany Transcendence and are inseparable from it.

The liturgy has adopted the Isaian hymn of the angels. With a profound appreciation of the fulfillment of the prophetic proclamations, it adds to it: "Blessed is he who comes in the name of the Lord." The liturgy recognizes that the Most High has come, and that He will come once again. It knows too that, in seeing Yahweh in the Temple, Isaiah had had the vision of the glory of Christ (Jn 12:41), for the glory of God has dwelt, since the incarnation and the Pasch, in the body of Christ, evermore glorious, in which Christians communicate by the celebration and reception of the Eucharist.[48]

[48] See Eric PETERSON, *The Angels and the Liturgy*, New York, 1964, pp. 30–40.

3. Let us go back five centuries. Moses, who has for the first time arrived at Sinai, to find refuge, sees something astonishing happen in a completely barren desert: a bush which, though it has been burning for some time, is not consumed. He comes closer.

"When the Lord saw that he turned aside to see, God called to him out of the bush, 'Moses, Moses!' And he said, 'Here I am.' Then he said, 'Do not come near; put off your shoes from your feet, for the place on which you are standing is holy ground.' And he said, 'I am the God of your father, the God of Abraham, the God of Isaac, and the God of Jacob.' And Moses hid his face, for he was afraid to look at God" (Ex 3:4–6).

Moses too is afraid. Once again, the place where God manifests Himself is awesome, unapproachable. Yet God *manifests Himself there*. Better: He calls. What we have here is the moment of the vocation and mission of Moses. And also the moment of the revelation of the Name of God:

"But Moses said to God, 'Who am I that I should go to Pharaoh, and bring the sons of Israel out of Egypt?' He said, 'But I will be with you. . . .' Then Moses said to God, 'If I come to the people of Israel and say to them, 'The God of your fathers has sent me to you,' and they ask me, 'What is his name?' what shall I say to them?' God said to Moses, 'I am who I am'" (Ex 3:11–14).

We know that this sublime text which records the reply of God can, grammatically, be translated in three—and even four—different ways. It can be translated, as was done by the Septuagint, as is done by the *Bible de Jérusalem* and by practically all bibles: "I am who am." God, asked by Moses to make known His Name, responds in what is surely a mysterious but nevertheless positive way. It is an answer which is in the sense of what

37

Etienne Gilson calls "the metaphysics of Exodus," the meta-physics of "aseity." But the text can also be translated: "I am what I am," "I am who I am." In that case, God refuses to answer, He does not give up His name, but retains its mystery. Finally, the text can be translated: "I will be who I will be [what I will be]," since the verb used in verse 14 is in the same tense as that in verse 12, where all bibles translate: "I will be with you." God here does not designate Himself as a nature, but as act: an act which is towards us, for us, with us, endlessly im-minent, endlessly before us. Who am I? You will see by my acts: I will be what you will see that I am when I free you from Egypt, when I feed you in the desert, when I lead you to Sinai to receive my Law and to enter into covenant with me, when I thus make of you my people, when I guide you to the Promised Land and bring you inside its borders. I will be He who dwells among you. I will be He who punishes you for your sins, who reduces you to nothing by defeat and deportation; He, also, who will free you, will restore you, will return life to you beyond destruction.

In these conditions, the living God, the God of faith, is cer-tainly He who, in the last book of Revelation, once more names Himself as "who is and who was and who is to come" (Rev 1:4, 8; 4:1; 11:17; 16:5). He *is* not merely (aseity), nor *was* He merely (eternity): *He is to come!* He is not merely in Himself, for Himself, in His transcendent perfection. He is for us, towards us, He is with us, opening to us the way of life and accompanying us as He who makes to be and to live.[49] "I will be who I will be," you will see it by my acts. Finally, in the fullness of time, at the

---

[49] Compare St. AUGUSTINE, *Enarr. in Ps. 101,* serm. II, n. 10 (*PL* 37, 1311): "Vade, *inquit,* et dic filiis Israel: 'Qui est' misit me ad vos . . . Ego sum, *inquit,* Deus Abraham, et Deus Isaac, et Deus Jacob (Ex 3:13–15). *Audisti quid sim apud me, audi et quid sim propter te . . .*"; *in Ps. 134,* 6 (*PL* 37, 1742–1743): "*Quod enim* Ego sum qui sum, *ad me pertinet, quod autem* Deus Abraham, Deus Isaac et Deus Jacob, *ad te pertinet. Et si deficis in eo quod mihi sum, cape quod tibi sum.*" But God, in what He is in Him-self and for Himself, is already what He wills to be for us. . . .

end of so many comings, of which none was total or definitive, I will be He who comes to you in person, who dwells among you, bodily. I myself will be your Pasch, I myself will be the passage through the Red Sea, I will be the true manna, the true bread of life, the true serpent raised in the desert, the true liberator, the true ransom for your sins, I myself will be the covenant with my people. I WILL BE JESUS CHRIST. For when God is not only "He who is, and who was," but also, in the fullness of His mystery, "He who is to come," His name is Jesus Christ. And He tells us: "You will die in your sins unless you believe that *I am*" (Jn 8:24).

The perfect reality of the living God, the God of Abraham, of Isaac, and of Jacob, the God of Moses, the God "who is and who was *and who is to come,*" in short, the *God for us,* is Jesus Christ, in whom "the whole fullness of deity dwells bodily" (Col 2:9). At Sinai, the apse of the Orthodox chapel, built very close to the place where Moses encountered God and received the Law, represents between Moses and Elijah, the burning bush. It is in the form of a circle giving forth flames surrounded by and mixed with green foliage. In the circle of flames, we see the Virgin with the Infant on her breast. It is thus that He who is appeared, in the place and at the moment when "*visibiliter Deum cognoscimus.*"

Towards a Return to the Living God

"*God everything to every one*"

It is clear that the God-for-us is the God of "the economy," and that all the acts of the saving economy are free and gracious. As such, they do not belong to the necessary mystery of God. Nevertheless, they do imply and reveal something of His nature. They are theophanic. Christmas, which itself involves the entire paschal mystery, from the Agony to Pentecost, and even to our final glorification; Christmas, which is the issue of the communications spread out through the course of salvation history, reveals that the Absolute is not only for Himself and in Himself, but is the Love-Gift, that is, *Agapē*. "God is Love" (1 Jn 4:8, 16). "In this the love of God was made manifest (*ephanerōthē*) among us, that God sent his only Son into the world, so that we might live through him" (1 Jn 4:9). There is no Absolute who is not at the same time Love, no "Great God" who is not the Good God, God towards us and for us.[50] There is no "I am," no *Ens a se*, no aseity, who does not bear within Himself not merely the possibility but the very bent towards being "I will be (for you, towards you, with you)"; there is no "He who was and He who is" who is not at the same time "He who is to come." Eternally, "He who is and He who was" is exactly what He became by coming to us. This is why "eternal life is that they know the only true God, *and Jesus Christ whom thou hast sent*" (Jn 17:4).

We have already pointed out that the economy necessarily involves questions of ontology: of divine ontology—we hardly dare pronounce such words, and do so only because there is a Word of God, in whose force we can attempt to mumble—and of general ontology as well. For if Being *a se* is *Caritas,* this must have repercussions in the ontology of all creation, and especially in the ontology of the creature whom He has made in His image. In the revelation of Being, something of the true nature of being is also revealed to us. Every study, every insight into what might be called the Christian or Judeo-Christian "specific" leads to the

---

[50] In June, 1958, a German mother told me, in Stuttgart, that her young child had asked her this question, vibrant with the most profound theology and completely disposing of Marcion's interpretation: "*Ist der grosse Gott auch der liebe Gott?*" Cf. St. IRENAEUS: "They [the Gnostics] think they have discovered a 'Great God' whom no one can know, who does not communicate with men, who does not rule earthly affairs. The God they thus have found is the God of Epicurus, a God who is of no use whatever, either for Himself or for others—a God without providence!" (*Adversus Haereses,* III, 24, 2: *PG* 7, 967).

question of the (Judeo-) Christian meaning of ontology. We have here a question of supreme importance, the very problem which Père Laberthonnière had posed (quite unhappily, though, since he burdened it with a lack of understanding and an un-healthy fear of scholasticism): the problem of a Christian on-tology, which can only be, as he said, an ontology of charity. We are convinced that this is true. Nevertheless, we must not tolerate the obstruction of stages which are and must be kept distinct. Before coming to charity, in which alone nature finds, by grace, its salvation (its meaning and its fullness), it would be well first to make some study of the Augustinian analysis of *esse-vere esse*, rediscovered or reëxpressed by Maurice Blondel in terms of degrees of being.[51] There is both the being of simple existence and the being which is rich, full, "consolidated." It is this latter which realizes the true relationship to Being. The finality, the relationship to the norm, the destiny of a being all enter into its integral ontological make-up, for one can *be,* but not *truly,* and one can be *truly.*[52] Heaven, that is, salvation, is realized when the relationship of beings, forming the whole of the universe, to Be-ing is perfect. St. Paul calls this state of things "God everything to every one" (1 Cor 15:28). And just as, in Judeo-Christianity, the term illumines the beginning, just as, biblically speaking, the truth of things is eschatological, so it is this which shows us the truth of all the ontological situations which are on this side of the ultimate ontological reality.

It is a metaphysical problem which is forced upon the mind: to know how there can be *beings* which are *apart from Being.* It is one of those "enigmas" of E. DuBois-Reymond; it is a ques-tion which Lachelier had asked. . . . It is clear that Being can refer only to itself, whatever of being might come to exist—let

[51] *L'Etre et les êtres,* Paris, 1936.
[52] T. BOMAN, *op. cit.,* well demonstrates that this is the biblical ontology and that it offers some agreement with a Platonic point of view (one of the reasons for the Platonism of the Fathers).

us not say, apart from it, but as distinct from it. As soon as Being posits beings distinct from itself, we must refer them and reduce them to it. The "Let the world be" of the beginning invokes the "God everything to every one" of the end. But the act by which the Absolute refers to itself is that by which it communicates being, life, happiness. There is no opposition. In it, there is identity between referring to itself and making happy. This is what makes so profoundly true the expression of St. Irenaeus: "*Gloria Dei, vivens homo, vita autem hominis, visio Dei.*"[53] The absolute *is* Love, and Love is Gift, communication.[54] The absolute is Generosity.

It is in Jesus Christ, in the coming of God in our flesh, that we recognize to what extent and in what way the Absolute is Love and Generosity. Not only, and not at the very first, as glory and victory, but at first as humility and abasement. Christmas, we have seen, is the beginning of that movement by which the Son of God, "splendor of His glory and the stamp of God's very being," reduces Himself to nothing, in the condition of a servant. The reference of everything to itself, whose realization Love, being Absolute, demands, is not effected immediately; but by means of an unimaginable condescension of the Absolute, He gives Himself up to this because He is Love. The relative will not be restored to the Absolute, nor will time to Eternity, creatures to the

---

[53] *Adversus Haereses*, IV, 20, 7 (*PG* 7, 1037). Biblically speaking, the glory of God consists in communicating His glory: Is 55:5; 62:7; Bar 4:37—5:1; Rom 9:22–23; Eph 1:18; 3:16; Col 1:27. On the problem which would be presented by an apparent opposition between the glory of God and *my* happiness, cf. H. DE LUBAC, "Le motif de la création dans 'L'Etre et les êtres,'" in *NRT*, 65 (1938), pp. 220–225; H. BOUESSÉ, "Théologie et Doxologie," in *L'Année théologique*, 11 (1950), pp. 193–212, 269–303; J. HUBY, "Salut personnel et Gloire de Dieu," in *Etudes*, 204 (September 5th, 1930), pp. 513–528.

[54] In his theology of the motive for the incarnation, St. THOMAS AQUINAS employs the principle whose formulation he borrowed from Denis, "*Bonum est diffusivum sui,*" IIIa, q. 1, a. 1. See C.–V. HÉRIS, *Le mystère de Dieu*, Paris, 1946.

Creator, beings to Being, without a descent of the Absolute into the relative, of Eternity into time, Creator into the creature, Being into the world of beings, the Holy One into the world of sin. The Absolute is Love to this extreme, the *Ens a se* is *Caritas* to this extreme. The condescension of God, as it is manifested in all the economy of His comings, and supremely in the kenosis of Jesus Christ, also has its *theo*-logical truth: in God, in the being of God such as the economy of salvation makes us know Him.

The whole history of humanity has been corrupted, has been broken, because Adam conceived a false notion of God. He wanted to be like God. I hope you have never thought that *this* was Adam's sin; what other ambition could he have? And is this not exactly what God had asked him to do? Adam simply chose the wrong model. He thought that God was an independent, self-sufficient being, and in order to become like him, he rebelled and disobeyed.

But when God revealed himself, when God wished to show what he was really like, he revealed that he was love, tenderness, effusion of himself, infinite kindness towards others, affection, subordination. God revealed himself to be obedient, obedient unto death. Whilst believing that he was becoming God, Adam became totally different from him. He entrenched himself in solitude, and God was but communion.[55]

What more could be added? Simply a conclusion whose theological and pastoral importance is, to our mind, very great.

Conclusions

The modern world, taken as beginning with the Renaissance, whose new anthropology has been analyzed by Dilthey and Cassirer,[56] resembles a man who is hard at work and even meeting with success, while quite unaware of a cancer which has not been detected by those whose job it is to care for him. He bears

[55] L. EVELY, *We Dare to Say Our Father*, New York, 1965, p. 24.
[56] W. DILTHEY, *Weltanschauung und Analyse des Menschen seit Renaissance und Reformation* (Ges. Schriften, 2), Leipzig, 1914, 3rd ed. 1929); E. CASSIRER, *The Individual and the Cosmos in Renaissance Philosophy*, New York, 1963.

within himself a tragic ambiguity, of which few Christians or few priests—the salt of the earth!—are conscious. The ambiguity consists in the separation of Love and Absolute. Love has been humanized, secularized, naturalized. We shall not go to the extent of saying, so as to deplore it, that *agapē-caritas* has become *humanitas*.[57] There was no need for it to become *humanitas*, because it was so already. Much rather should it have stayed so! Christmas remains forever the day "when the goodness and loving kindness of God our Savior appeared" (Tit 3:4). The truth is, as Jacques Maritain has explained in his *True Humanism*, that modern humanism does not consist in a discovery of the human following upon a long misunderstanding of man, but is a kind of humanism *minus* God and the incarnation, by a non-theologal humanism.

It can be said that the modern world, completely centered on man as it is, has developed a *humanitas*, a "philanthropy" purely human and earthly, not theologal. But Christians, for their part, had somehow lost the sense of the inclusion of the *humanitas* or "philanthropy" of God in the theologal. From then on, the "theologal" was no longer the theologal of the Absolute who is Love. It tended to become a theologal of cult, yes, a cult, a duty paid to an Absolute thought of as throned on high, in a sort of celestial Versailles. This process is discernible in the religion of the classical era such as it evolved, while still preserving much grandeur and vitality, after 1660 or so; then, in that, more moralized and humanized still, which was expressed in the eighteenth century; and, finally, in that of the least mystical or apostolically committed religious circles of nineteenth-century bourgeois society. It would take us too far afield, were we to demonstrate this by adducing the necessary proofs.

This separation of what God had however united has had ex-

<hr/>

[57] This is one of the themes developed in M. FUERTH, *Caritas und Humanitas. Zur Form und Wandlung des christlichen Liebesgedankens*, Stuttgart, 1933.

tremely serious consequences. When we look for the doubts, the objections, which constitute, for many of our contemporaries, a kind of stumbling block on the road to faith, we always come, though by different routes, to the same difficulty: "God—so what? I prefer ordinary men to churchgoers. Religion is nothing but a superior, a subtler egotism. What has religion to do with work, with the reality of the human couple, with the problems, large or small, of real life?"

Men want a humanity without God because, as Yahweh expressed it to Samuel, "they have not rejected you, but they have rejected me from being king over them" (1 Sam 8:7). Part of the reason, also, is that we have too often presented them with a God who lacks "philanthropy," with a theology which did not call at once for an anthropology, with a first commandment which could very well do without the second. . . .

The solution, to the extent it depends on us, is not to increase our bid with regard to man and the world. It lies in a return to the full truth of the Living God, the God of the Bible and of faith, the God of salvation history. There is nothing more urgent than doing all we can to know and to make known the *true* God, the God whose last name is pronounced Jesus Christ.

Appendix

Extracts from patristic texts on the theme:
Christ, the revealer of "God"

Clement of Rome, *Letter to the Corinthians,* 36, 2: "Through Him [Christ] we see, as in a mirror, His [the Father's] spotless and sublime countenance"; 59, 2: "Through Christ, God has called us to pass out of shadows into light, out of ignorance into the knowledge of the glory of His name."

Ignatius of Antioch, *Letter to the Ephesians,* 19, 3: "Ignorance was dispelled, the former kingdom destroyed, when God appeared in the form of man for a newness of eternal life."

Polycarp, bound to the stake to be burned (*Martyrium Polycarpi,* 14): "O Lord, Almighty God, Father of Jesus Christ, your well-loved and blessed Son, who has taught us to know you. . . ."

Irenaeus, *Adversus Haereses,* III, 6, 2 (*PG* 7, 861): "Thus through *the Son* who is *in the Father* (Jn 14:10–11) was *manifested* the *Father bearing witness* to the Son and the Son announcing the Father. As Isaiah again says (43:10): 'And I am the witness, says the Lord God, I and my Son whom I have chosen, that you may know and believe and that you may understand that it is I.'"

III, 11, 5 (*PG* 7, 883): ". . . the God *who made the earth* and who commanded it *to bring forth fruit,* who *created the waters* and *made the springs gush forth,* this very God in these last days gives to the human race the blessing of Food and the favor of Drink, through His Son—God 'incomprehensible'

46

through Him who is 'comprehensible,' God 'invisible' through Him who makes 'visible.' . . ."

IV, 6, 5–7 (*PG* 7, 989–990): "*Et ad hoc Filium revelavit Pater ut per eum omnibus manifestetur, ut eos quidem qui credunt ei justi, et incorruptelam, et in aeternum refrigerium recipiat (credere autem ei est facere ejus voluntatem).* . . . *Omnibus igitur revelavit se Pater, omnibus Verbum suum visibile faciens.*" No. 7: "*Et sine illo [Filio] nemo potest cognoscere Deum. Agnitio enim Patris, Filius, agnitio autem Filii in Patre, et per Filium revelata, et propter hoc Dominus dicebat: 'Nemo cognoscit . . .'* (Mt 11:27)."

V, 1 (*PG* 7, 1120–1121): "We could not otherwise have learned what are the things of God, if our Master, being the Word [of God], had not become man. For no other could have told us the things of the Father, unless His own Word: 'For who has known the mind of the Lord, or who has been his counselor?' (Rom 11:34; Is 40:13)."

In the *Epideixis*, 92 (*Patrologia Orientalis* XII, 796), Irenaeus applies to the incarnation the text of Isaiah 65:1, "I appeared [I made myself visible] to those who sought me not. . . ."

Clement of Alexandria, *Paedagogus* 1, 7, 57, 2 (ed. Staehlin, Leipzig, 1905–1909, I, 124): "Christ is the visage [*prosopon*] of God"; other references in M. Harl, *Origène et la fonction révélatrice du Verbe incarné*, Paris, 1958, p. 77, note 25.

Origen, *In Joan.*, 6, 32 (*PG* 14, 821–822): the Son glorifies the Father by making Him known.

De Principiis, 1, 2, 8 (*PG* 11, 136): "*Verbum quoniam non solum splendor gloriae esse dicitur ab Apostolo, sed et figura expressa substantiae vel subsistentiae ejus.* . . ." Why is Christ so called? Because He reveals the Father. But there is something more: the eternal equality of the Word with the Father.

Contra Celsum, 1, 97 (*PG* 11, 1145).

Anaphora of Serapion 1, 3 (from the French translation in *Dictionnaire d'archéologie chrétienne et de liturgie*, XI, 609):

"We praise you, you who are known by the only-begotten Son, by Him revealed, explained, and made known to created nature."

Athanasius, *De Incarnatione Verbi,* chs. 4, 16, 45, 46 (*PG* 25, 120–121, 124–125, 176–177, 177–180).

Hilary, *De Trinitate,* V, 20 (*PL* 10, 142, 143): "God is seen, and God speaks of God whom He has seen. God cannot be understood except by God."

John Chrysostom, *In Joan. Hom.* XII (*PG* 59, 81–84); *Hom.* XV (*PG* 59, 97–102), Christ the image of the invisible God (Col 1:15); God, invisible even to spiritual creatures, made Himself known in the flesh (1 Tim 3:16).

Cyril of Alexandria. *In Joan.,* I, 10 (*PG* 73, 177); XI, 1 (*PG* 74, 461); XI, 3 (*PG* 74, 493–496); XI, 7 (*PG* 74, 500). Jesus made God known *as Father.*

Leo the Great. *Sermo* XXVI, 2 (*PL* 54, 213).

To conclude, let us add references to the following studies: F. Amiot, "Deum nemo vidit unquam: Jo. 1, 18," in *Mélanges bibliques A. Robert,* Paris, 1957, pp. 470–477; J. Alfaro, "Cristo Glorioso, Revelador del Padre," in *Christus Victor mortis* (*Gregorianum,* vol. 39), Rome, 1958, pp. 222–270; R. D. Luckhart, "Matthew 11:27 in the Contra Haereses of St. Irenaeus," in *Revue de l'Université d'Ottawa,* 23, pp. 65–79 (1953); R. Latourelle, "L'idée de révélation chez les Pères de l'Eglise," in *Sciences ecclésiastiques,* 11 (1959), pp. 297–344 (from St. Ignatius Martyr to St. Augustine, inclusive); A. Van der Bosch, "Le mystère de l'Incarnation chez saint Bernard," in *Citeaux,* 10 (1959), pp. 83–92; 165–177; 245–267 (Majesty and condescension); *Id.,* "Dieu devenu connaissable dans le Christ d'après saint Bernard," in *Collectanea Ord. Cisterc. Ref.,* 22 (1960), pp. 11–20; "Le Christ, Dieu devenu imitable d'après saint Bernard," in *ibid.,* pp. 341–355.

Second Part

Our Mediator

1

What Jesus Learned

CHRIST'S infused knowledge and acquired learning. —From
Nazareth to Golgotha. —The incarnate Word became "doctor"
of men. —Jesus, the perfect prophet.

Christ's Infused Knowledge and Acquired Learning

Christ, true God, is also "true man." As such, He learned many
things by education, by experience, and by all the exchanges
which make up the texture of every life in human society. St.
Luke, when he was writing of Jesus as a child, says that He "increased in wisdom and in stature, and in favor with God and
man" (Lk 2:52; cf. 40). We can find many statements of this
kind in the Gospels: "When Jesus *learned* that the Pharisees . . ."
(Jn 4:1). We have no intention of compiling a list of the texts
which imply, in Christ, a passage from ignorance to knowledge
by means of instruction, experience, or reflection. Neither do we
intend to look for a theoretical or theological explanation of the
fashion in which this register of knowledge, a human register, is
in harmony, both as to substance and as to manner of acquisition,
with the other registers of knowledge that scholastic theology
identifies in Christ: "infused knowledge," human still as to its
substance, but supranatural as to its manner of acquisition;
"beatific vision" of the divine Essence and of all things "in the

51

Word." . . . The problems which this involves are difficult indeed, and we can find in their discussion the sum total of theological reflection on the mystery of the incarnation. We refer the reader to the studies devoted to them. Their number, never complete, grows larger every year.[1]

What we propose is something less ambitious, although it is still a matter of theological reflection and of our knowledge of Jesus Christ, the Saviour of men. We would like to study the contribution to the execution of His mission as Saviour of the world which was made by the knowledge Jesus acquired during His human life, whether by education, experience, relationships with other men, or, finally, by His human reflection about the world, men, and God. Our meditation will principally bear on two points: the experience Jesus had as a child in His family life,

---

[1] The theology of the schools is represented by St. THOMAS AQUINAS, *Summa Theologiae*, IIIa, qq. 9 to 12; this remains basic, but the research and discussion of the last few decades show that it is not the last word. Can it, for example, be held, with St. Thomas (q. 9, a. 4, ad 1; q. 12, a. 3), that Christ was not instructed? —We can cite: F. VIGUÉ, "Quelques précisions concernant l'objet de la science acquise du Christ," in *RechScRel*, 10 (1920), pp. 1–27; J. LEBRETON, *History of the Dogma of the Trinity. From its Origins to the Council of Nicaea*, New York, 1939, vol. I, pp. 417–432; A. DURAND, "La science du Christ," in *NRT*, 71 (1949), pp. 497–503; A. MICHEL, article "Science du Christ," in *DTC*, XV, cols. 1626–1665, and *Ami du Clergé*, 1960, pp. 641–649; J. TERNUS, "Das Seelenbewusstseinleben Jesu," in *Chalkedon*, vol. III, Würzburg, 1954, pp. 81–237; J. GALOT, "Science et conscience de Jésus," in *NRT*, 1960, pp. 113f.; E. GUTWENGER, *Bewusstein und Wissen Christi. Eine dogmatische Studie*, Innsbruck, 1960; C. CHOPIN, *Le Verbe incarné et rédempteur* (Le Mystère chrétien), Paris, 1963, pp. 81f., 93–102; *Problèmes actuels de Christologie*, Paris-Bruges, 1964; *Gott in Welt* (*Festgabe für Karl Rahner*), Freiburg, 1964, vol. I, pp. 608f. A *status quaestionis* of current research in Christology can be found in A. GRILLMEIER, "The Figure of Christ in Catholic Theology Today," in *Theology Today*, Milwaukee, 1964, pp. 66–108; in R. HAUBST, "Probleme der jüngsten Christologie," in *Theologische Revue*, 52 (1956), cols. 149–154; in *Revue des Sciences philosophiques et théologiques*, January, 1963, pp. 99f. (*Bulletin de Théologie dogmatique: Christologie*, by B.-D. DUPUY). —Questions touching on the knowledge of Christ had been much discussed, either in the Anglicanism of the late nineteenth and early twentieth centuries, or during the years of the modernist crisis (cf. E. POULAT, *Histoire, Dogme et Critique dans la crise moderniste*, Paris, 1962, vol. I, pp. 485f.).

and the bearing of Christ's experience on the revelation He made, on the fulfillment, which He initiated, of the true religious rapport, that of the new covenant or the Gospel.

From Nazareth to Golgotha

Christ's filial obedience

Jesus merited and made satisfaction in His humanity, above all by His acts of love and obedience, acts which He drew from within His human heart, in the face of sufferings so many and so great that they tended to turn Him away from them. These acts are freely distributed throughout His earthly life, but their substance was, one might say, summed up in the hours of His passion: at the Cenacle, at Gethsemani, on the cross. . . .

During our lifetime, there are certain acts in which we sum up years and years which were seemingly ordered to them in advance. The soldier who has readied himself in body and in mind, sometimes over a long period and at a great distance, for the moment of battle, sums up years and years of training and practice in a few minutes, which are critical and well may be his last. The religious who pronounces his vows sums up, in a few instants, all the fervor and fidelity of many years of self-giving, prayer and obedience. In the second it takes to say the "yes" which joins a bridegroom and bride for their married life together, there are summed up not only many months, perhaps many years, during which was formed, increased, expressed and strengthened a love which extends to the determination of a total and definitive mutual giving, but also all the preparations by which this young man and this young woman have become what they are and have formed in themselves the foundations of the love and fidelity which they now mutually exchange. The "yes" which they pronounce derives its strength and truth solely from the strength and truth, in a word, from the *quality* of the years which, since childhood days, have made ready the soil and vigor. These too are the years which are summed up in the "yes" of a decisive day.

When Jesus knew (by "infused knowledge" and by the experience of the events in which the drama was developing and gradually reached its resolution), when Jesus, then, "knew that his hour had come to depart out of this world to the Father, having loved his own who were in the world, he loved them to the end" (Jn 13:1), Jesus summed up all the love for His Father and for men which from the very beginning had animated His coming into the world. "Now is my soul troubled. And what shall I say? 'Father, save me from this hour?' No, for this purpose I have come to this hour" (Jn 12:27). Everything has been tending towards this hour, everything has prepared for it, everything is going to be consummated in it. It is the moment in which everything which had been formed, unfolded, expressed, in the soul of Jesus, of love for the Father and for men, of filial obedience to His Father, would be summed up in the supreme acts of the passion, from which life would come to us.

He had already prayed, "Thy will be done" (Mt 6:10, and parallel text). "My food is to do the will of him who sent me" (Jn 4:34). "For I have come down from heaven, not to do my own will, but the will of him who sent me" (Jn 6:38; cf. 5:30; Heb 10:7-10). And now that "the hour" had come, He entered willingly upon the painful road that His Father had decided, and He prayed: "My Father, if it be possible, let this cup pass from me; nevertheless, not as I will, but as thou wilt" (Mt 26:39, 41; Mk 14:16; Lk 22:42). All the filial obedience of Jesus is summed up in His passion, by which our salvation is effected. He had practiced it throughout His life and, by this very practice, He had humanly better understood and deepened it. He had been trained by His parents and He had learned it from them, just as He had learned from them, and from His teachers, and from His

Jewish background, love and respect for the Temple,[2] religious and other basic acts, prayer, the Psalms, the primary import of Passover and of the feasts which, by the witness of St. John, He was to make the context of so much teaching, of so many messianic acts.

In this way, the human feelings, the dispositions of heart and of will, by means of which Jesus effected our salvation, had gradually been formed in His experience as a young Jew,[3] and in His education at Nazareth by Mary and Joseph.

This had been an education to prayer, to love for God, to obedience towards Him. But, actually, the great religious attitudes, all of them simple and profound, are prefigured in the attitudes which we acquire towards our parents and our relatives, towards other men, and also towards the homeland whose heritage we must accept and honor. The Jewish rabbis used to say that the fifth commandment (our fourth), the one which commands us to honor our father and our mother, had been written on the first tablet of the Law because the love and respect which we give to our parents is still love and respect to God. St. Paul was to say that disobedience and lack of respect towards parents were characteristic of a world which is pagan or which has once more become pagan. . . .[4]

The submission of Jesus to His parents is the sole trait by which St. Luke, who brought together the memories which Mary had stored up in her heart, describes the years during which Jesus grew up and received His training (Lk 2:51). We are familiar with the technique of ancient authors, who, in telling of the life of their hero, were interested only in those facts which

2 Cf. our *The Mystery of the Temple,* Westminster, 1962, pp. 112f. Cf., e.g., Mt 23:16f.; Mk 11:16–17.

3 Cf. R. ARON, *Jesus of Nazareth. The Hidden Years,* New York, 1962.

4 Cf. Rom 1:20; 2 Tim 3:2. On filial piety as the basis of a psychology of respect and delicacy, there are very rich and profound pages to be read in Pierre Célestin LOU TSENG-TSIANG, *La rencontre des humanités et la découverte de l'Evangile,* Paris, 1949, pp. 49f.

bore a relationship to his mission or public destiny. They did not look, as we tend to do today, for minute details and curious incidents, but for the signs which were an indication of the great destiny to come. What St. Luke is writing is a sacred history, a page from salvation history; only that is retained which is relevant to the salvific mission of Christ. This point is crucial. Jesus learned obedience, not only through what He suffered, as the Letter to the Hebrews (5:8) tells us, but also from His life as a child in His home at Nazareth. It was by the practice of the fourth commandment that Jesus began, in His human soul, the practice of filial obedience which He had to give to His heavenly Father. It was this which began the formation in Him of the sentiments and the attitudes by which, in His passion, He effected our salvation. Péguy understood this in a way which is indicative of the measure of his appreciation of Christian things:

Last of all, or rather over and above this, Jesus not only as it were doubled, not only consecrated, *authorized* (and even crowned), not only ratified, not only revitalized the fourth commandment by clothing Himself in obedience and filial submission, *et erat subditus illis;* He, over and above, He, last of all, brought the fourth commandment to its full realization, to its supernatural omnipotence. For the obedience, the submission of Jesus to His foster parents, so perfect in itself and of eternal instructive value, were still only a temporal image, a carnal representation of the eternal fiilial obedience of Jesus to His Father *who is in heaven.* The obedience, the day-after-day submission of Jesus to Joseph and Mary heralded, represented, anticipated the awful obedience and submission of Holy Thursday.[5]

Yet we must bring to an end this quite impressive view of the filial soul of Jesus. Yes, His loving obedience to His Father in heaven was first formed, in His human consciousness, by His

[5] Charles PÉGUY, *Un nouveau théologien, Monsieur Laudet,* § 111, Paris 1936, p. 34. Péguy adds (n. 45, p. 35): *"Tunc venit ad discipulos. Et dixit.* It is precisely this thirty years' apprenticeship, this submission, this patience, this obedience for thirty long years, for every day of a thirty years' apprenticeship, preparatory, introductory to the submission, the patience, the obedience of the last day, that M. Laudet cuts away from us as *not belonging to us at all."*

child's attitudes at Nazareth. But within the unity of His Person, which existed with the existence of the Word, the awareness which Jesus had of the man who was for Him His father, the just and humble man of Nazareth, was enlightened by the intuitive knowledge which He possessed of the mystery of God and of what paternity is in God, of which any human paternity is only a reflection (cf. Eph 3:14). Walter Dirks has shown that the representation of the father, or the substance of the notion deriving from it, was changed, between antiquity (or even the ancient Jewish world) and our time, by the fact of the revelation which was made, by Jesus Christ, of God as the perfect Father.[6] Previously, the father had principally been seen as power, albeit a tutelary and provident power. Since then, we have known that he is love and mercy, without ceasing to be absolute Origin and Authority. Our knowledge of the heavenly Father has as much, and even more, clarified our notion of earthly fathers, as the latter has served our religious appreciation of the paternity of God.

It thus comes about that, in the conceptual and verbal material through which we can know and name God, the contribution of man and his experience and the contribution of God, which reveals something of His mystery, correspond, in a kind of dialogue, and condition one another to form the *Christian* understanding and judgment. Before we can name God as Father, even before revelation can propose Him to us under that name, we must have recourse to the idea, however poor, which we have formed of "father" out of our experience of men whom God has made, however remotely, in His image. Then we can apply that idea to

[6] *The Monk and the World,* New York, 1954, pp. 128–130. The case of St. Thérèse of the Child Jesus is most significant: the formation of her idea of the divine paternity did not start *from* her father, nor her idea of spiritual childhood *from* the childhood images which she employs solely to express herself; their formation starts from the personal mystery of God, communicated and lived. Cf. André COMBES, *Saint Thérèse and Her Mission,* New York, 1955, pp. 202–204.

God. This is the role of the holy and humble "analogy of being." But—and this is important—the use which God makes of these terms in His Word, as He uncovers something of His purpose and of His being, illuminates, expands, enriches and confirms, as well, the lowly and deficient notion which He expects us to derive. This is an astonishing exchange, and, in the last analysis, we are the sole beneficiaries of it.

This exchange was first effected in the human consciousness of Jesus as a child. As His love and obedience towards His heavenly Father were being nourished by the love and obedience which He showed His father and mother, there was occurring an illumination of the developing idea of His father and of the substance of the name He would so often utter when speaking of God. This illumination stemmed from the vision which He had, at the summit of His most holy soul, of the very Face of the Father who is in heaven, the Father whose name He had to hallow, whose will He had to do, with such great fervor. We are speaking of these things as well as we can, yet we are able to do no more than hint at the infinite depths of the human soul of Jesus Christ, the ineffable exchanges which took place there between the perfect light which came from God and the mumblings of a human intelligence which then was really but that of a child. . . .

"O the depth of the riches and wisdom and knowledge of God!" (Rom 11:33).

The Incarnate Word Became "Doctor" of Men

Jesus, says St. Thomas Aquinas, acts in two ways to communicate salvation to us: through His teaching and through His causality. He not only effects salvation—we have seen the role played there

---

7 "*Per modum causae, per modum doctrinae,*" "*faciens, docens. . . .*" Cf. *I Sent.,* d. 16, q. 1, a. 3; *In Joan.,* c. 1, lect. 11 (at the beginning); c. 4 lect. 1.

58

by His human attainments—but He teaches the Gospel. This is the totality of His activity as "prophet" or doctor, as revealer of the mysteries of God. What role, in this activity of preaching the Good News (cf. Mt 1:1), is played by all that Jesus acquired through education, experience and reflection, on the level of His human consciousness?

To begin with, there is the part played by His dialogue with men. The Gospel is, in good measure, set forth within the pattern of exchanges, which sometimes took the form of appeal, sometimes of question-and-answer, sometimes of confrontation and conflict. Now Jesus knew the thoughts of hearts (cf. Mt 9:2; Mk 2:8; etc.); "he needed no one to bear witness of man; for he himself knew what was in man."[8] Even so, we often see Jesus asking questions (cf., e.g., Mt 16:13). Was this simply a pedagogical technique? There certainly is such a pedagogical technique, but we find here that the reaction freely expressed by men, as it is received by Jesus, conditions the revelation which Jesus makes in replying: He "answers," He carries on what His interlocutors have begun. . . .

Jesus, the initiator of the new and definitive disposition of the covenant, must reveal the religious rapport in all its truth. In order to do this, He must reveal something of the mystery of God and of the true state of man, and also of the state to which man is called. Jesus did this by drawing unceasingly not only from the treasure of human knowledge and language, but also from the experience which He acquired from things and from men. Much more was involved, from His standpoint, than a pedagogical technique through which He could bring to the comprehension of His listeners a knowledge obtained in a superhuman fashion, by direct illumination. Certainly, that was there,

---

[8] Jn 2:25; compare 1:48, in regard to which the *Bible de Jérusalem* remarks: "Supernatural knowledge of men and of events is one of the characteristics of the Johannine Christ: cf. 2:24; 4:17, 19, 29; 6:61, 64, 71; 13:1, 1, 27, 28; 16:19, 30; 18:4; 21:17."

but there was also, in the mind of Jesus, revealer of the things of God, an active, and even developing, understanding of the revelatory power of the realities which He had, as man, learned of or experienced. We would like to show how this is true with regard to three orders of knowledge: the lowly realities of the world of men, the texts of Scripture, and certain religious realities lived by the people of God.

Jesus' exercise of His mission of revealing the things of the Kingdom started from a total and true human existence: it is the Word *made flesh* who is the doctor of men. He who had come to make the name of God known to men (Jn 17:6, 26), did not cease to think about His mission, as He looked at things, learned their names and properties, as He walked among men. Unceasingly, He sought and found in them all the power they possessed to signify what He had to make known. He bent over with ardor into the chalice filled with flowers so as to draw from them the signifying element of the thought of God which is to be found at the heart of things and which must, somehow, be brought forth. If the grace of the poet lies in revealing to men that there is a "presence," accessible to them, in the realities of the world, that these realities have something to say to them, Jesus was surely the great poet of the world and on the basis of a sublime poetics He revealed God.

What He told us about His Father, who takes care of His children (cf. Mt 6:26–32) and who would no more refuse the gift of the Holy Spirit than our fathers would give us a stone when we asked for bread (Mt 7:9–11; Lk 11:9–13), incorporated the experience which He had had of human parents and of His own father. The sight and experience of so very many humble things even supported the parables of the Kingdom: we do not put a piece of unshrunk cloth on an old garment, nor new wine into old wineskins (Mt 9:14–17; Mk 2:21–22; Lk 5:36–39); a lamp we put on a lamp-stand (Lk 8:16ff.; 11:30ff.); we

60

ke the trouble to look for something which has been lost, and
hat joy there is when it is found! (Lk 15). Jesus saw the sower
oing forth to sow (Mt 13:3ff.; Mk 4:1–9, 13–20; Lk 8:4ff.),
e had been present when men were being hired (Mt 20:10),
e had seen the yeast being put into the dough (Mt 13:33; Lk
3:20–21), and so many other familiar activities which were for
im analogies of the mystery of the Kingdom. . . . It was while
e was observing all these things that He, as revealer of God,
ad nourished His thought and had prepared Himself to draw
om His treasure both the new and the old (Mt 13:52).

Jesus had little to do with the schools of the learned (cf. Jn
:15)—this was why the exceptional quality of His preaching
used so much surprise.[9] Yet He had not any the less studied
e Scriptures, either in His home at Nazareth, or in the ele-
entary school, such as was affiliated with every synagogue, or
Himself, in His own prayer and meditation, during the years
 manual labor (cf. Mk 6:3) and of His evangelical ministry.
his acquired knowledge entered into the warp and woof of His
fe and preaching, though without prejudice to infused knowl-
lge or to immediate revelations. Thus it is that He had recourse
 the Scriptures to repulse temptation, to reply to the Phari-
es.[10] When, after His resurrection, He explained to the disciples
erything which concerned Him in Moses, the psalms and the
ophets (Lk 24:25ff., 44ff.), He was referring to texts which He
d read and re-read, just as had been done by those to whom He
ished to explain them.

At the same time that the soul of Jesus was being enlightened
 the knowledge which the Father directly communicated to
im of His design of salvation and of the way to accomplish all

[9] Mt 7:28; 13:54–57; Lk 2:47; 4:22; Jn 7:46. Compare, in regard to the
ostles, Acts 4:13.
[10] Mk 2:23f. (David and the bread of the Presence); Mt 22:41–45; Mk
:15–17; Lk 20:41–44 (David calls the Christ his "Lord"); Lk 20:17
pplication of Ps 118:22, "the stone which the builders rejected").

that had been foretold, His soul was acquiring, through medi‹
tion, a deeper understanding of the texts which had spoken
Him. Everything which He would one day explain to the discipl
on the road to Emmaus, or in other circumstances, and whi
would be the foundation of the apostolic exegesis, referring ever
thing to Christ and to the Christian mystery, Jesus at first b
understood as much by reason of His meditation as by reason
the enlightenment received from His Father. This understandi‹
was rooted in His human knowledge of the Scriptures, followi‹
Abraham, Moses, David, the prophets, and all those who h
"looked for the consolation of Israel" (cf. Lk 2:25). Jesus h
been the first to read and to understand the Scriptures in ref‹
ence to Himself. He had understood Himself as, and had, so
speak, revealed to Himself His role as the holy Servant foretc
by Isaiah. He did this in the measure that He meditated on t
sacred texts, and then in the measure that everything was bei‹
fulfilled. His consciousness coördinated the lights that it receiv‹
within the different "registers" to which we have referred, a
attained the absolute fullness of meaning of the Scriptures and
the design of God. This was to be the measure of all that t
Church, following the apostles, would understand and wot
communicate in her tradition,[11] whose dogmatic content is pr
cipally, according to the witness of the Fathers, the true Christi
understanding of the Scriptures.

The same process of Christian understanding was also appli
to the great realities which were lived by the people of God a
which Jesus was to bring to their full truth, in the newness of ‹
Spirit.

We are thinking especially of the Pasch and of the Temp
but we also have in mind the Law, the priesthood, the sacrific

[11] This extremely profound idea has been developed particularly by En‹
MERSCH, S.J., *The Theology of the Mystical Body*, St. Louis, 1952; *Le Chr*
l'homme et l'Univers, Paris, 1962; and by Canon Jean MOUROUX, *1*
Mystery of Time. A Theological Inquiry, New York, 1964.

the covenant. . . . All of these now found their truth in Jesus. He knew this, and He said this. He died to give witness of this. But, before that, He had nourished His knowledge of these holy realities by His faithful practice of them, in communion and solidarity with His people. Thus, when He announced, and later effected, the definitive truth of the Pasch and of the Temple in the mystery of Himself, Jesus put into this all the substance which sustained Israel, while awaiting Him without knowing Him: in celebrating the Pasch, in frequenting the Temple, in the intense fidelity brought to the observance of the Law, in offering the sacrifices which Jesus was to consummate in a single sacrifice. All the fervor which God had communicated to His people as it awaited the new Wine, Jesus assumed when He changed the water of Cana into wine, when He celebrated for the last time the Pasch with His own and introduced the sacrament of the new and definitive Pasch. What He had learned, experienced, and understood, as a child, then as an adult, in the practice of the Jewish religion, entered, as the sketch into the completed work, into the revelation and the institution of the new covenant which He contained within Himself.

Jesus, the Perfect Prophet

We have shown the role of the human, moral, and intellectual acquisitions of Jesus in the acts by which He was our redeemer and in the acts through which He was, for us, the revealer of the Father and of worship in spirit and in truth. We found in them all the truth of the incarnation. The incarnation is not limited to the fact, somehow ontological or (meta)physical, of the hypostatic union, but is realized in a human history whose full human truth is necessary to its own. This is why real sufferings, real acquisitions of learning, real progress in this learning, a real assumption of the experiences undergone by Jesus as a child and as a member of His people, had to enter into the acts by which

63

Jesus Himself would be the revealer of God and the redeemer of men.

But Jesus is Man-God. He possesses a teaching authority[12] and a power of operation[13] which do not come to Him from this human register, but enter, nonetheless, into His work of revelation and redemption. Among the different registers on which Jesus can play, there occur interpenetration, interchange, cooperation whose concrete modalities escape us. If He had not had knowledge, received immediately from God, of the full truth which He had to reveal, Christ would not have known, with the necessary fullness and assurance, the signifying value of the human notions and words of which He had experience. If He had not known the Holy Spirit, He would not have known that water is a powerful symbol thereof. . . . It was necessary that there be some irruption in Him of the light of the creative Word for Him to know, at the level of His human consciousness, the revelatory value, the power to reveal God, possessed by the images of which He, like us, was aware.

This thoroughly supernatural wisdom also allowed Him to know man with all the profundity necessary to appreciate that the humble notions and the simple words He used would be the adequate and truly inexhaustible nourishment of men, not only until the end of the world, for all the coming centuries of experience and discovery, but also for man's deepest being. What Dostoevski says of the three temptations: "For in those three questions the whole subsequent history of mankind is, as it were, brought together into one whole, and foretold, and in them are united all the unsolved historical contradictions of human nature,"[14] Jesus truly knew in solid and final fashion. This was no less true of all His words. In them is to be found the principle

12 Cf. Mt 7:28–29; Mk 1:22; Lk 4:22, 36.
13 Countless texts: Mt 28:29; Jn 3:35, with the note in the *Bible* de *Jérusalem*.
14 "Legend of the Grand Inquisitor," *The Brothers Karamazov*, Part I, Book V, Chapter V (Constance GARNETT translation).

64

of eternal life, of absolute life and truth (cf. Jn 6:38). The prophets had brought to men words whose significance was more profound than they realized, words which were true as if beyond themselves, and forever. But Jesus *knows* the importance and the infinite value of His words and deeds: yes, of His *human* words and deeds. He knows it by that knowledge directly communicated from God and by that direct vision which, in consummating His human knowledge, result in making of Him the perfect prophet.

His human knowledge furnishes to His mission of revelation, not only a pedagogical store of images, but also communicable content, analogies, and points of departure. His infused knowledge, His direct vision of the mystery of God and of His design, illumine His knowledge with the light that confers on it the certitude and power which make it authentically revealing. This union, this symphony, is demanded by the economy of communication of Himself and of salvation which God chose to establish: an incarnation in Jesus Christ, true God and true man.

2

God Reveals Himself in Poverty[1]

THE mystery of the poor. —Our way to God passes through the poor. —The poor in the mystery of the incarnation.

The Mystery of the Poor

The first thing that impressed us was that God reveals Himself in poverty. We see this in the election of Israel, the people which was the bearer of the revelation. It was not because Israel was powerful, or because it stood out as a creative force in the cultural field, that it was chosen as beneficiary and witness of the revelation. Israel was, on the contrary, small, and it was because of its smallness that it was chosen (see Deut 7:7; cf. 10:14–15; Ezek 16:3–15; 1 Cor 1:27). Within Israel itself, those who were chosen to be bearers of the design of God were those whom neither superior qualities nor preëminent position marked out. On the contrary, it was the youth who were chosen in preference to the elders (see the story of Cain and Abel, Jacob and Esau, Ephraim and Manasse, David . . .), it was the sterile who became the mothers of the great chosen ones of God: Sarah,

[1] Report presented during the council to the group of bishops studying the theme, "The Church of the Poor," under the chairmanship of Cardinal Gerlier of Lyons. The report was based on the work of a team inspired by Père Paul Gauthier, of Nazareth, which dealt with the theological aspects of the question.

Rebekah, the mother of Samson, Hannah the mother of Samuel, Elizabeth the mother of John the Baptist, finally Mary the mother of Jesus, who proclaims:

He has regarded the low estate of his handmaiden, . . . he has scattered the proud in the imagination of their hearts, he has put down the mighty from their thrones, and exalted those of low degree (Lk 1:48–52).

The history of souls and the witness of spiritual men speak in a fashion which is so much in agreement and which is so categorical that it seems necessary for us to consider as a law of the spiritual world, one as certain as the laws of the natural world, the necessity to be and to recognize oneself as wholly without resources, so that God might lift us to Himself. Yes, truly, He fills the hungry with good things and sends the rich empty away (Lk 1:53). Is it because God is sovereign and wishes to be affirmed as such? He who exalts himself before Him (so much the more, he who exalts himself against Him), He brings low;[2] he who acknowledges his poverty before Him, He fills.

In all of this, poverty is not a question of a purely material condition. Between the Pharisee and the publican, it is rather the publican who would, in the economic sense, be found to be a possessor. The ideal is not to be in want, but to be free in the face of abundance or of privation, as was the Lord Jesus or St. Paul (cf. Phil 4:11), and, especially, to have in one's soul the attitude of waiting and of desire, of openness to grace, of dispossession, of total and confident dependence which is the attitude of "The Poor of Yahweh" (see Albert Gelin's beautiful book of that name, Collegeville, 1964). Material poverty, destitution, a humbled condition constitute no more than *dispositions* which may be favorable; but they could also set up reactions of bitterness and envy, revolt and rejection, which would be as contrary to the Gospel as the hardness of heart, the self-sufficiency, the ingrati-

[2] Reread on this subject Is 2:6–22; Zeph 3:11.

67

tude, and the pride of a wealthy man who is dispensed, by his wealth, from putting his confidence in God. We do, nevertheless, very often find among the poor (the *Misérables* of Victor Hugo, and also those of Tolstoy, Gorky, . . .) the dispositions of non-possession, of welcome and of sharing which are, as if naturally, acknowledged as proper to the Gospel. The only thing lacking to these dispositions is that they have not been evangelized, have not even been recognized as a religious attitude. Jesus Christ would have to be shown to these poor ones. He is the fullness of all that is already in His image.

The next thing that struck us was that the poor can be re-vealers of God. They can be a means or a way of finding Christ. We are, in fact, held back from finding this way by our attach-ment to certain goods, certain false pretensions, by the snare constituted by comfortable habits, by the fear of risk. But when we confront the poor, when we come into contact with them, our false security and our illusions melt like snow in the sunshine. The "glorious" and utterly vain creatures we have made of our-selves strike us as hollow and false. We take stock of the fact that, after all, we knew nothing: we were empty, we were not even apprentices. Then, if we have a touch of nobility in our hearts and some small beginning of spiritual unrest, we see our-selves as judged and we judge ourselves; we are very close to hearing the voice of truth.

Very quickly, though, we came to see that there was, on the part of Jesus, a certain predilection for the poor, that there was a certain identity, confirmed by His own words, between Himself and them.

It is quite true that we cannot, in the name of the Gospel, somehow canonize poverty in the economic sense of the word. If this were required, we would have to maintain men in that condition of poverty. But, as the Fathers, the theologians, and the popes have often said, the Gospel does not require that the poor exist so that the rich can practice mercy: it would be far better if there were no poor![3] The Gospel does not canonize material poverty. Still, one cannot reduce its message to an exaltation of poverty *in spirit*. Certain facts, certain statements resist any such process. Jesus Himself chose first to lead a laborious life, then a poor life, without assurance of resources. And the apostles too, to whom it was said: "Blessed are you poor" (Lk 6:20), were next told: "Blessed are you that hunger now, for you shall be satisfied." Then there followed the curses which correspond, term for term, to the beatitudes: "But woe to you that are rich, for you have received your consolation. Woe to you that are full now, for you shall hunger." The particular insistence of St. Luke on poverty in the social sense of the word is quite well known. Still, we cannot exclude this aspect from the fourfold witness which was inspired by Him whose Gospel we know it to be. We must see it in its place. . . . It is also difficult to attempt to understand only in a spiritual sense the terms used to express the messianic sign. "To preach good news to the poor. . . , to proclaim release to the captives, and recovering of sight to the blind" (Lk 4:18; Is 61:1). The help brought to the unfortunate seems inseparable from the spiritual liberation, exactly as so many miracles show us that it was in the life of Jesus.

The parable of the wicked rich man and Lazarus is also proper to St. Luke (16:19–31). He does not say "the *wicked* rich man", nor does he say that Lazarus was a "poor man" in the spiritual sense of the word. Lazarus was, quite simply, a poor man, and it was on this basis that he received consolation. We can, therefore, ask whether there may not be, in the Gospel, a predilection for the poor as such.[4]

[3] Cf. St. AUGUSTINE, *In Epist. Joan.*, tr. VIII (*PL* 35, 2038).
[4] Compare the following remarks of Père Benoit: "I take the word 'poor' in a broad and realistic sense, covering not only those who are economically deprived, not only the pious souls, humble and trusting in God, of whom the Old Testament freely speaks, but also everyone who is unhappy or un-

Better still: in the teaching about the last judgment which is given in St. Matthew (25:31–46), Jesus identified Himself with the poor: "I was hungry and you gave me food. . . , I was naked and you clothed me. . . . As you did it to one of the least of these my brethren, you did it to me. . . ." The just were not aware that, in doing these acts of charity, they did them for the Lord Himself. He was, then, really hidden under the appearance of the hungry, the naked, the imprisoned. . . .

And yet, we can wonder if the teaching really goes that far. Does it affirm the general fact of an objective presence of Christ in the poor, so that in going to them we encounter Him? Or is the affirmation more detailed, more limited? Many commentators are of the opinion that the works of mercy involved—known and recognized as such in the biblical milieu[5]—are to be exercised towards other *disciples:* "to one of the least of these *my brethren.*"[6] We can cite in support of this opinion well-attested parallels: "Whoever receives one such child in my name receives me" (Mt 18:5; Mk 9:37; Lk 9:48; cf. Jn 13:20; Mt 10:40ff.). There would then be question of nothing more than the revelation of a proper and crucial characteristic of the Christian ethic: our acts involve a vertical relationship to God or to Christ. The text of St. Matthew on the judgment would, then, do no more than reveal this dimension of Christian behavior and apply it to acts duly recognized as done for the benefit of other Christians, members of the mystical body.

---

fortunate in the eyes of men, the sick, the crippled, the ugly, whether in body or in soul or in mind, the despised, the rejected, the disreputable, and, of course, the sinners. For these, Jesus has a pronounced predilection. He seeks them out, He commits Himself to their company. He pursues them so as to save them physically and morally" (in *L'Evêque dans l'Eglise du Christ,* Paris, 1963, p. 360).

[5] Cf. Is 58:7; Job 22:6f.; Sir 7:35; Ezek 18:7, 16; Heb 13:2, 16; Jas 1:27. For the spiritual works of mercy, see Rom 12:12–16; Gal 6:1–2; Eph 4:1 and 32; 1 Thess 5:14–17.

[6] Thus, St. THOMAS AQUINAS, *In Matt.,* c. 25, n. 3; E. MERSCH, *The Whole Christ. The Historical Development of the Doctrine of the Mystical Body in Scripture and Tradition,* Milwaukee, 1938, pp. 60f.

Even then we could question the way in which "the least of my brethren" was being interpreted. These words can, in fact, signify, not the special quality of disciple, but the general fact that all men were considered by Jesus as His brethren and that, among them, the "least", that is, the poorest, the most oppressed, the most despised, were particularly His brethren. This, we think, is the true meaning of the text. On the level of a theological reflection, it must be understood within the basic fact of the Incarnation, as we shall see further on. Let us go forward gradually in an attempt to probe the reasons for the existence between God (Christ) and men, especially between God and the disgraced and the needy, of a connection of such a nature that an encounter with the latter has the value of an encounter with God, and that the charity which is practiced on the human level has the value (we hardly dare say it!) of good done to God. . . .

Our Way to God Passes through the Poor

"What you did to one of the least of these . . ."

Actually, we could even go so far as to speak of the role of things and events in this regard. Even things which are alive, but not spiritual or personal, bear vestiges of God. Man, however, bears His image. If we do no more than consider the framework of an existence in which God is in search of man and man, even without knowing it, is ordered to find God, we see that everything is, in some degree, an occasion for an encounter with God, a place for a possible visit. Everything has an "iconic" value, one to which the saints were particularly sensitive, and which Jesus perceived to the highest degree.[7] Things are parables in potency, presenting the possibility of signifying the religious rapport and of inducing its realization. The universe, the things and the events

---

[7] See, within, the chapter on "The Preaching of Christ."

within it, all can become sacraments of the active presence of God.

Looked at from the standpoint of our advances, there is a continuity, and thus a homogeneity, between the attitudes we assume in our encounters with things (which are, after all, the context of our decisions and contain in a real, even if latent, way the occasions for encountering God) and the fundamental attitude we assume towards God Himself. The latter attitude is foreshadowed in our habitual and basic decisions, but gradually takes shape in the exercise of our freedom, within a field of successive and mutually conditioned advances: of God towards us, and of us towards God, advances which vary according to every possible degree, every possible modality of clear or obscure awareness of what is at issue.[8] What is important to our present reflection is that we be conscious of the encounter with God which takes place under the guise of something other than God, that we be conscious of the connection and continuity which exist in this area. This very connection and continuity have their reality in God Himself, in whose sight we are, and in whose regard we, when confronted with creatures or events, choose.

We can assume that what is generally true of our encounter with things is true also, in particular conditions, of our encounter with *persons* or with *men*. This seems to us to be true for two principal reasons.

By reason, first, of the mystery which every person contains. We never know *who* we are encountering. Abraham sees three men coming towards him. He shows hospitality to them. Yet the sequel of the story shows that they were three angels, three messengers of God, or even God Himself in person (cf. Gen 18 and 19:1). . . . Simon of Cyrene, coming back from the fields to

8 We have explained this kind of dialectic of approaches which alternate while conditioning one another, in the chapter cited in note 7, and in *The Wide World, My Parish. Salvation and Its Problems*, Baltimore, 1961, pp. 99f.

make ready the Pasch, is forced by Roman soldiers to take up the cross of a condemned man who could not carry it to the end. Did he grumble, or did he accept the task with a good heart? Later, it will be made clear and his sons will be found among the Christians (cf. Mk 15:21). At the moment he did not know that he was helping the Son of God to carry the instrument of the world's salvation. We could give example after example to prove that we never know *who* we are encountering, *who* is sent to us, *who* we receive. . . .[9] This is true in the most special way for us who are priests. What exactly is the man looking for who knocks on my door, who sits down next to me on the train? What is in the soul of the man who comes to arrange for a wedding, the fellow who asks to confess his sins? Who are they? And how many times have I been blind and deaf, callous and dense, incapable of even suspecting, of even guessing! . . . Yet everything witnesses to the mystery of hospitality, of openness. The word "mystery" is not too strong a word here, since it indicates that there is something beyond what is seen, something in which God is working and can be attained. . . .[10]

However that may be, the man whom we encounter is *a person*. This is why he lends himself in a formal way to becoming the occasion for us to declare our attitude towards God, who is *Person*. There is no other creaturely mediation which can do this in the same way. These persons are, morever, made in the image of God, and this makes of them a reflection, an echo, somehow a prolongation of God. "For we are indeed his offspring" (Acts 17:28). When we learn from the Word of God that the second commandment is like to the first, we realize to what extent it is

[9] I have referred elsewhere to the following story, which was told me by one who had been present. An Italian priest who had come to France to take up a collection for his projects sought hospitality in a Paris rectory. When Don Bosco was canonized—for it had been he—one of the priests who had welcomed him said: "If we had known that he was a saint, we would have given him the best room, rather than the attic. . . ."

[10] On the subject of hospitality, see Jean DANIÉLOU, "Exile and Hospitality," in *The Lord of History*, Chicago, 1958.

73

true that, in the persons of other men, we reach God Himself. It might even be said that, in a certain sense, we cannot fully realize the love of God except in the love of neighbor. St. Catherine of Siena said that "we conceive the virtues in the love of God, and we bring them forth in the love of our neighbor."[11] We could apply this maxim to theologal love itself, inasmuch as love, by its own nature, wills to procure the good of the one who is loved. It cannot content itself with being affective, but wills to express itself and to prove itself in good works. But what am I to bring to the Lord that He does not have already? The love which I have conceived for Him has, we might say, its *locus* in the world in the love I have for my neighbor. In this kind of created extension of God in His living images, I can do Him the good that is demanded by my love for Him. In this sense, God has, so to speak, given me my neighbor to love in His place. . . . In the Gospel revelation, not only does the love of God seem linked to the love of neighbor, but it is somehow enveloped by it.[12] In the Sermon on the Mount, Jesus expresses the evangelical demands with regard to God (Mt 6:1–18) only after He has expressed those which concern the fraternal relationship with regard to one another (5:21–48). That this sequence is not due to editorial happenstance, that it translates the sense of the Gospel doctrine, can be seen in ten places where it is clearly shown in particular applications, most notably in the law which governs forgiveness (Mt 6:12; 18: 21–35; Lk 6:36–38).[13]

If God became man in Jesus Christ, this fact cannot possibly be without influence on the role which is played by humanity,

11 JORGENSEN, *Saint Catherine of Siena,* New York, 1938, p. 130.

12 On this point and on what follows, see H.-M. FERET, "Peuple de Dieu, mystère de charité," in *La Vie Spirituelle,* October, 1945, pp. 242–262; "Charité et Vérité," in *L'Eglise, éducatrice de la charité. Congrès de l'Union des Oeuvres,* Lyons, 1950. Paris, 1951, pp. 53–106.

13 Cf. G. MARTELET, "Remets-nous nos dettes. . . ," in *Verbum caro,* no. 38 (1956), pp. 79f.

74

hence by men, in the religious rapport. We think that there are two points which must be emphasized here:

1. In Jesus Christ, God has united Himself to human nature, which is really one; He has thus made of all men His brothers. The divine decree which decides the redemptive incarnation brings about, between men and Christ, a particular solidarity, one which corresponds, besides, to what is called for by the very nature of the realities involved.[14] In virtue of this solidarity, Jesus, God-made-man, draws men to form with Him a single subject, entitled to the heritage of God (provided men receive the gift of God through a personal and free act of living faith). This constitutes the foundation of the people of God under the new dispensation, which makes of this people the Body of Christ. The solidarity which God effects brings with it this consequence: what is done to men is done, in a certain way, to Christ. Where disciples and the body which is the Church are involved, this solidarity is translated in the "Saul, Saul, why do you persecute me?" of Acts (26:14; 9:5; 22:8). This is the most intense degree of mystical identification. In the least explicit degree, anything which is done to any human person whatever touches Christ. Within the area between the two degrees, we would undoubtedly have to situate all that might be done to the Jews. But, if our reading of the text from St. Matthew is correct, the truth is that there is, on the basis both of the decree of God and of the existential conditions of the incarnation, a particularly solidarity, a certain "juridical identification"[15] between Christ and all those

[14] The aspect of free *act of God* is signified, in Mt 25, by the expression, "The blessed *of my Father.*" When we speak of the nature of the realities under discussion, we have in mind, on the one hand, the unity of human nature, and, on the other, in decisive fashion, the hypostatic union, from which there flows necessarily the following consequence: Jesus the man becomes, for all human nature, the principle of restoration, a re-formation of the distorted image, and, at the last, a divinization.

[15] The expression is Théo PREISS's ("The Mystery of the Son of Man," in *Life in Christ*, London, 1954, pp. 51–60).

75

who are in need of help: the poor, the hungry, the imprisoned, the lowly. . . .

2. "God's love (*agapē*) has been poured into our hearts through the Holy Spirit who has been given to us" (Rom 5:5). The love of which this text speaks is, as we know, the love with which God loves. In fact, the sublimity of charity is such that it represents a participation in the love with which God loves Himself and all things. When we profess that we love our neighbor "for the love of God," our profession means nothing else and nothing less. Now the love with which God loves us has assumed a way and a form which have given it a definite character and, in doing that, have revealed its deepest nature. "I am the way," says Jesus, "no one comes to the Father, but by me" (Jn 14:6). Yes, He *is* the way, the living way which He has opened for us through His flesh (cf. Heb 10:20). We know what this way, as the unique path of truth and of life, has been, and we know what it will forever remain: the way, humble and filled with love, of service of men, the way of a descent right down to the brambles to seek the sheep that is lost, right down to the dust of the earth to seek the lost coin. To love with the love with which God has loved us? This is to love as Jesus loved (and this is the "as" which is demanded by the *new* commandment, *His* commandment . . .). It is to love with a love which seeks with predilection the little ones, the ones who are in need. . . . All of this is bound up with the *newness* of the Gospel, which itself is the consequence and the reflection of the mission, inspired by the *agapē* of the Father, of the Son of God. "The great revelation of His Gospel is the boundless love of Himself and of His Father for the little ones whom the world scorns or condemns. When we know of the mistrust of Judaism—and of so many 'self-respecting' religions—for these 'unclean ones,' we sense the full revolutionary character of the attitude of Jesus. We are already aware of the scandal of the Pharisees when confronted with a salvation which was too easy and was offered to every comer. Qumran now pro-

76

vides us with an even clearer example of this scrupulous *intégriste* piety, which thinks it is better to serve God through an isolation from all that is not itself and through a hatred for sinners."[16]

When determining the place of all these factors in the plan of God, one cannot avoid making the following statements: the way that leads to God passes through the humanity of Christ, something which is inseparable from the love and service of men, particularly those who are in misery under all its forms. If it is true to say, with Saint John of the Cross, that "in the evening of this life we will be judged on love,"[17] it is more certain still that we will be judged on the basis of this: "As you did it to one of the least of these my brethren, you did it to me." The aim of the preceding meditation has only been to try to better understand this saying of our Master. We have seen that it supposes, between men and Christ, a link of such a nature that all men, and particularly the poor, enter as decisive elements into the realization of the religious rapport.

We first saw the poor as an occasion, a sort of sacrament of the encounter with God. We even saw them as identical, in a certain manner, with Jesus Christ. Our way to God passes through them. . . . What we would like to do now is to prolong our meditation by considering things from the point of view of God and of Christ. We will no longer ask ourselves why men, and especially the poor, play a decisive role in the religious rapport or in evangelical behavior. We will ask, instead, what it is, from the standpoint of Christ and of God, that links them particularly to the unfortunate. What has Christ to do with the poor? What is the basis, in God and in Christ, of the kind of predilection which we have observed? It is in Christology that we must seek the

[16] P. BENOIT, in *L'Evêque dans l'Eglise du Christ,* Paris, 1963, p. 360.

[17] "At eventide they will examine thee in love." "Spiritual Sentences and Maxims," no. 57, *Complete Works of St. John of the Cross,* trans. and edited by E. Allison Peers, Westminster, 1957, vol. III, p. 247.

light which will best illumine an entire aspect of the Gospel and, as a corollary, an entire aspect of the mission and life of the Church as well.

The Poor in the Mystery of the Incarnation

If the incarnation implies a structure which is in some way metaphysical or ontological—the subsistence of a human nature in the hypostasis of the Word, it remains, before all else, a fact of "the economy," the disposition of the will of God as it is gradually unfolded and realized in time, of which St. Paul speaks in the Letter to the Ephesians (1:3–14). The incarnation is not dependent on the necessary mystery of God, but on His free mystery. It is not dependent on the "in Himself," but on grace, on what God freely decides to be and to do for His creature. The fact that God decides to become man and the concrete circumstances or modalities chosen by God to effect this design represent positive data which are absolutely free in themselves but, once decided on and effected, present the believer with something which he must understand and imitate. This is the order of the mysteries of the economy. It is what the holy Scriptures are talking about when they say that *it was necessary that this be accomplished: "Oportebat pati Christum,"*[18] *"ut Scripturae implerentur."*[19]

We have here an order of realities which, considered from

---

[18] This "it was necessary" refers particularly to two orders of events: a) the passion of Christ and certain of its circumstances: Mt 26:54; Mk 8:31; Lk 9:22; Lk 17:25; Jn 3:14 and 20:9 (the resurrection); Acts 17:3. —b) The trials encountered in the struggle for the Reign of God: Acts 14:21; the preaching of the Gospel: Mk 13:10; the coming of Elijah: Mk 9:10; the woes: Mt 24:6; Mk 13:9; Lk 21:9; certain details of what must take place during the militant stage of the Reign of God: Rev 1:19; 4:1; 22:6.

[19] With very few exceptions (Mt 13:35; Lk 4:21 and 21:22), these statements have reference to the passion: Mt 26:54; 27:9 and 35; Mk 14:49; Lk 22:37; 24:44 and 46; Jn 18:9; Acts 3:18; 13:27. —Jn 12:38 and Acts 1:16 are connected with the passion, which thus appears as the central fact of salvation history.

78

logical reason alone, is a free order of simple fittingness, but which, in the existential context of the purposes of God and the saving economy, is imposed upon us as a law of Christian activity. Moreover, reason, seeking an understanding of what we believe (*fides quaerens intellectum*), discovers in it marvelous and profound harmonies. The actual order of the economy then appears as so astonishingly coherent, both as to the unfathomably profound nature of God and as to the profound nature of man, in the light of his present condition and of the end that is promised to him, that the *oportebat* or the *necesse erat ut Scripturae implerentur* seem filled with light and logical order.

God, indeed, *is* Love, God *is* Grace. Grace is freedom, but its very impulse as grace makes of it a condescension and a gift which intimately correspond to the aspirations and the nature of love. Its reality as grace brings it about that God can be as well in what is low as in what is high. "How could God's deity exclude His humanity," writes Karl Barth, "since it is God's freedom for love and thus His capacity to be not only in the heights but also in the depths, not only great but also small, not only in and for Himself but also with another distinct from Him, and to offer Himself to him?"[20] He whom the heavens, whom the most sublime created spirits cannot comprehend or contain, can dwell in the lowest without its being burst asunder or destroyed.[21] The Old Testament said: no one can see God without dying. But when God made Himself more intimately known by coming to us Himself, by becoming one of us Himself, we knew for certain that it is by seeing Him and by touching Him that one has life (cf. Jn 14:9; 1 Jn 1:1f.).

But if grace, through its character of freedom and transcendence, dwells with the low as well as with the sublime, we are

---

[20] *The Humanity of God,* Richmond (Va.), 1960, p. 49.
[21] Compare St. GREGORY THE GREAT: *"Omnipotens Deus, qui nec in magnis tenditur nec in minimis angustatur . . ."* (*In Ezech.,* lib. II, hom. 2, 15: PL 76, 957B); still more, the *Imago Primi Saeculi* of the Society of Jesus: *"Non coerceri a maximo, contineri tamen a minimo, divinum est."*

79

forced to say that its profoundly loving and condescending nature actually inclines it to come to the lowest and the most miserable. Everything which has been said about *agapē,* the gracious love of God, must be repeated here. And everything that can be said about the kingly character of mercy as well.[22] There is then in grace, and in God inasmuch as He is *agapē* and *grace,* not only some possibility of being with the smallest, but an actual inclination to go to the poorest, to the one who is most miserable, so as to communicate to him His Good and His Life. Everything which we have, thanks to the book of Anders Nygren, re-assimilated on the theme of *agapē* was implied in this: it is not by reason of a goodness possessed by someone whom the *agapē* loves, but, on the contrary, *because* someone is poor and miserable, that the *agapē* loves him. Reread in this connection 1 Jn 3:16; 4:9; Rom 5:8 and 8:32–39; Eph 2:4–7; Jn 3:16.

Now all that God is in His profound being, and especially all that God is *for us,* all that He is as grace, has been supremely manifested to us in Jesus Christ.[23] But, at first, God did not make Himself known except from afar, and through an intermediary. One day, He came Himself. In Jesus Christ, He freely manifested Himself: "Philip, he who has seen me has seen the Father" (Jn 14:9). But how, and in what form? It is here that the *"oportebat," "ut Scripturae implerentur"* take on all their force. When God freely manifests Himself, when He definitively reveals to us the way of truth and of life, the way which is His, the way which is Himself, what do we see?

1. He does not remain a stranger to misery. He did not assume sin, but He did assume and bear the consequences of sin: He joined men, He married our humanity in the conditions of our misery, largely conditioned by sin. It is undoubtedly true

---

[22] See "La Miséricorde, attribut souverain de Dieu," in *La Vie Spirituelle,* April, 1962, pp. 380–395 (reprinted in *Les Voies du Dieu vivant,* Paris, 1962, pp. 61–74).

[23] Cf. *supra,* pp. 1f.

that we cannot simply attribute to sin all the miseries of men. Misery makes its own chain of being. There are certain factors, inherent in the nature of things, which by themselves create the conditions of misery: poor soil and subsoil can hardly yield anything but poverty. Man, though, is called to free himself and to free others from misery, and sin prevents this. Sin is always the exaltation of self to the detriment of others, egoism, self-justification, refusal to share and to act as a servant in love and in self-surrender. It is also the worship of idols, of the false absolutes fabricated by men, and all the ignorance and alienation which that brings with it. Even Christianity has been and sometimes still is thus bent, although this is the complete contrary of faith in the living God, the God of the incarnation and of the Pasch. As for the history of the world, it is a history made up of the trampling of the weak by the strong, the crushing of the little by the great, and, for the majority of men, the incredible accumulation of woes.

At Christmas, we pray: *"Ut nos Unigeniti tui nova per carnem nativitas liberet:* that the *new* birth in the flesh of your only-begotten Son *free* us."* These phrases are all but paschal in character. The beginning of our liberation consisted in this: He who was in the light, the riches, and the glory of God (Jn 17:5) began to exist among the little, the poor, the lowly. . . . He became a little child, weakness; He was born in a working-class family and He Himself worked with His hands; He grew up among a people subjected to a military occupation, under authorities who made no game of submission; He knew what it was to be hungry, to be in pain, to be held in suspicion, to be put on the index by the most sacred authorities; He knew contradiction; He knew, finally, the conditions of total destitution of a man accused, the defenseless exposure to accusations and to blows, to flagellation, to the horrible punishment of the cross, a punishment imposed on slaves. When we meditate on the circumstances of "the blessed passion" of Christ, we cannot help thinking that Jesus

81

assumed it all so as to be fully *with* so many poor people who, throughout the ages, have been beaten, hanged, crucified (the five thousand slaves crucified after the revolt of Spartacus; the five hundred Jewish patriots whom Josephus claimed to have seen crucified at once). . . .

2. The incarnation is not the pure metaphysical fact of the assumption of a human nature in the uncreated subsistence of the person of the Word. It is existentially a fact which was produced in such and such concrete circumstances, announced, anticipated, prepared for a long time, then finally realized: *"oportebat," "ut Scripturae implerentur."* Now what do we find?

We find Jesus announced as the suffering Servant.

We find him avoiding the title of "Son of David," which would have suggested the idea of a kingship of a human type, and taking the title of "Son of man." He rejects the prospects of triumphal or temporal messianism which are set before Him either by the Tempter, or by the crowds, or by His disciples and His brethren: He will be liberator by the cross, He will overcome misery by assuming it.

The most profound revelation touching on the incarnation is given to us by St. Paul in the Letter to the Philippians, 2:6–11. The fact which we celebrate on March 25th and December 25th is there presented as the beginning of a descent, even as a "kenosis," a making-into-nothing. Yes, the beginning: to come as a tiny little child—the weakness, the total dependence which is a little baby!—is but the beginning of a descent which will only be accomplished *at the lowest point* of human existence, death. The term of the "kenosis" of Christ is the descent to hell, a very profound mystery which is essential to our faith and by which our faith takes on all its human and cosmic dimensions, its depth and its realism.[24] The Eastern tradition, and the icono-

[24] Some references for a study: C. CLEMEN, *"Niedergefahren zu den Toten." Ein Beitrag zur Würdigung des Apostolikums,* 1900; K. GESCHWIND, *Die Niederfahrt Christi in die Unterwelt. Ein Beitrag zur Exegese des N.T.*

graphy which it inspired, is particularly impressive here. On the one hand, the Greek Fathers and the liturgy present the incarnation as the commitment to the movement of abasement which will go as far as death and the descent to the abode of the dead (cf. above, note 11); the liturgy indeed announces the feast of Christmas under the title of "Pasch, holy day of three days' duration."[25] On the other hand, the Eastern icons of the resurrection are not, as they are among us (Matthias Grünewald, etc.), historically oriented representations of the departure from the tomb, with the guards either asleep or thrown to one side (a point of view which is quite naturalistic, very external): they are principally representations of the descent into hell (see the works by H. J. Schulz and W. Bieder which are cited in note 24). In these icons, Christ is shown at the lowest point on the cosmic journey which is referred to in the Letter to the Ephesians (4:8–10): "In saying, 'He ascended,' what does it mean but that he had also descended into the lower parts of the earth?" Jesus not only descended into the lowest places, that is to say, the earth in opposition to heaven, but even into the lowest places of the earth. He descended to the very lowest point. It is then, starting from there, and in such conditions, that He will accomplish the second stage of the "journey of cosmic scope" (P. Benoit)

---

und zur Geschichte des Taufsymbols, 1911; D. PLOOG, *De descendus in 1 Pet. 3, 19 en 4, 6* (1913); A. GRILLMEIER, "Der Gottessohn im Totenreich," in *Zeitschrift für Katholische Theologie,* 71 (1949), pp. 1–53, 184–203; O. ROUSSEAU, "La descente aux enfers, fondement sotériologique du baptême chrétien," in *RechScRel,* 40 (1952), pp. 273–297; *Id.,* "La descente aux enfers dans le cadre des liturgies chrétiennes," in *La Maison-Dieu,* no. 43 (1955), pp. 104–123; E. BISER, "Abgestiegen zur Hölle. Versuch einer aktuellen Sinndeutung," in *Münchener Theol. Zeitschrift,* 9 (1958), pp. 205–212, 283–293; H. J. SCHULZ " 'Höllenfahrt' als 'Anastasis,' " in *Zeitschrift für katholische Theologie,* 81 (1959), pp. 1–66; M.-H. LELONG, "La descente aux enfers, épiphanie aux morts," in *La Vie Spirituelle,* 100 (1959), pp. 17–28. For the iconography, see W. BIEDER, *Die Vorstellung von der Höllenfahrt Jesu Christi. . . ,* Zürich, 1949.

[25] See Th. SPASSKIJ, "La Pâque de Noël," in *Irénikon,* 30 (1957), pp. 289–306; A. NOCENT, "Cette Pâque qu'est Noël," in *Feu nouveau,* no. 6 (December, 1962), pp. 24–29.

83

of which St. Paul speaks. Its result will be to permit Him to "fill the entire universe." It is the second stage and it consists, no longer in descent, but now in ascent: *"Ho katabas autos estin kai ho anabas. . . .* He who descended is he who ascended."

This is exactly the same logic, the same economy, that we find in the great rhythmic text, perhaps a Christian hymn, of the Letter to the Philippians, 2:6–11. Adam, who existed in the condition of servant, yielded to the temptation to raise himself above his own condition to attain a condition of God, and imagined himself as an absolute independence, without subjection to anything ("You will be like God, knowing good and evil": Gen 3:5); but Christ, who existed in the condition of God, did not remain covetously attached to this dignity, but took the condition of slave, which is the condition of men, and in this very condition He abased Himself to the extent of suffering, in our place, the punishment of slaves, the frightful death of the cross. This is why God exalted Him to the extent of making Him Lord over all that He has encompassed, from the highest to the lowest.

Glory is promised to us with Christ, provided we first suffer with Him, says St. Paul (Rom 8:17). We must enter into the law which constitutes the most specific part of the Christian ethic and which has us act as Christ—or, rather, as God has shown us, in Christ, that He acts: to love *as* He loved, to pardon as He pardoned, etc. The great text from Philippians opens with these words: "Have this in mind among yourselves, which was in Christ Jesus." In this "marching in the footsteps," we are in the earthly phase, at the stage of descent and of service. To be obedient to the Christian law, which has its own intrinsic obligation (*oportebat*), is to be born with this new birth, whose final goal is liberation, which means to descend to the lowest, to begin to exist with the poor.

The poor are not only the economically deprived; they are not only the poor "in spirit." They are all those who suffer misery, in the broadest extension of the word. This extension corresponds to the sense in which Christian tradition has looked at misery: it has acknowledged the spiritual works of mercy along with the corporal, and it has practiced them, but it has not yielded to the error of believing, for all practical purposes, that either can do without the other.

3

The Prayer of Christ

THE witness of the New Testament. —The Our Father sums
up all the prayer of Christ. —Prayer, communion in the mystery
and in the will of God. —Jesus, center and summit of universal
prayer.

The Witness of the New Testament

"We must pray without ceasing"

St. Ambrose, commenting on the verse of St. Luke (6:12): "In
these days he went out into the hills to pray; and all night he
continued in prayer to God," points out: "He prayed alone.[1]
Nowhere, unless I am mistaken, do we find that He prayed
with the apostles. Everywhere, He implores alone. The reason
for this is that the design of God cannot be grasped by human
desires, and no one can have part in the intimate thought of
Christ."[2] As we begin our meditation on the prayer of Jesus, it
is good to recall that all the actions of the incarnate Word are

---

[1] On the prayer of Christ, St. THOMAS AQUINAS, *Summa Theologiae,* IIIa,
q. 21; Adalbert HAMMAN, "La prière de Jésus-Christ," in *Bible et Vie
chrétienne,* no. 10 (May-July, 1955), pp. 7–21 (reprinted in *La Prière
depuis les origines chrétiennes jusqu'au Concile de Nicée,* Paris, 1959).

[2] *In Lucam,* V, 43 (*PL* 15, 1733).

86

mysteries.[3] The religious intelligence can and does receive great lights on these mysteries, but quickly senses that it will never be able to exhaust their content or understand their profundity. No matter how far it goes, it will never do more than begin to understand something which surpasses it. In the thought of a great genius, there always remains something to be understood beyond what one grasps. But here there is much more besides. Here we are seeking to comprehend actions which surpass all human experience and knowledge, for they are actions of a man who, in saying "I pray" or "My Father," is using an "I" and a "my" which really refer to an absolutely infinite divine Person.

Nonetheless, it is as man, and with a fully human prayer, that Christ prays. The New Testament speaks quite fully to us about His prayer, so that, while revering the mystery, we can attempt to penetrate those areas of the prayer of Jesus which are thus made clear and accessible to us. We will do this by putting ourselves first in the presence of the fact, massive and yet detailed, of this prayer and, then, by making more precise the relationship which we, who pray so poorly, have with the prayer of Jesus Christ, our Lord.

What the Gospels, the synoptics in particular, tell of the prayer of Jesus is always detailed. It is linked with a precise act or moment in the accomplishment of His work.[4] More than one text, of course, shows us the Lord as praying simply to pray;[5] but even these moments, in the Gospel accounts, appear connected to certain precise episodes: Mark 1:35 shows us Jesus withdrawing to pray in solitude, but it is before He leaves to preach the Good News. Mark 6:46 (and Mt 14:23) describes

---

[3] St. AUGUSTINE, on the weariness of Jesus (Jn 4:6): *"Jam incipiunt mysteria . . ."* (*In Joan. Ev.,* tr. XV; *PL* 35, 1512).

[4] Parallel observation in A. GEORGE, " 'L'Heure' de Jean, XVII," in *RB*, 61 (1954), pp. 392–397 (394).

[5] For example, Mk 1:35; 6:46; Lk 5:16; 9:18; 11:1. To these should be added the prayers of thanksgiving (Mt 11:25; Lk 10:21; Jn 11:41; 12:29) and the wholly interior, unexpressed prayer. . . .

Him as going to the mountain to pray, but He does this just before the storm which will be quelled only by His presence. St. Luke's text (6:12), with which we began this article, immediately precedes—we can even say that it introduces—the choosing of the Twelve. Luke 9:18 says: "Now it happened that as he was praying alone the disciples were with him; and he asked them, 'Who do the people say that I am?' . . . ," and we are given Peter's great confession which, in St. Luke, does not imply the same ecclesiological and dogmatic fullness as in St. Matthew. Luke 11:1 says simply: "He was praying in a certain place," but it was then, at the request of a disciple, that Jesus taught His prayer, the Our Father. We could go on: in Luke 9:28–29, the prayer of Jesus—an absolute prayer, a prayer for the sake of praying—introduces His transfiguration. We will soon come to the prayer of Jesus during His passion.

There are further testimonies, Luke 5:16, for example, which show us, in Jesus, a life of continual prayer, led for its own sake: "But he withdrew to the wilderness and prayed." We also see (*supra,* Lk 9:18) that certain episodes intrude on a life of continuous prayer which is independent of them. The testimony of the Gospels requires us to see Jesus as given to prayer in an extremely intense way. It does, however, uncover for us the mystery of this prayer within the thread of a revelation of the economy of salvation. Our Gospels do not speak to us of the prayer of the Lord in this way because they are stories, rather than studies of psychology or spirituality, but because they wish to tell us what we must know in order to live, on the basis of faith, the religious rapport of the new and eternal covenant. The soul of Jesus is revealed to us principally in what it is *for us,* His life in what He did *for us.* Of all that Jesus was in respect to His Father, the Gospels tell us what we must know so that we might be, after Him and through Him, the children of that Father who will be invoked, in His prayer and in ours, under that very title.

The Gospels almost always give in some detail the external circumstances of the prayer of Jesus. The places, first of all. We never read that Jesus came to the Temple *to pray.* Unquestionably, this does not rule out the possibility that He did pray there, but we are never told of it. On the contrary, He is there shown to us as *teaching,* as carrying on the service of the Gospel for which He came, exactly as He did in the synagogues.[6] Neither do we ever see Him there offering sacrifice, or taking part in an exercise of worship. When He comes to institute the sacrifice of the new covenant, He will do it outside the Temple, in a house. And He Himself will offer His sacrifice outside the Temple, even outside the city, raised on a cross in the sight of all, so that, as St. Leo says, the mystery of the former victims being abolished, a new victim might be placed on a new altar, and the cross of Christ might be the altar, not of the Temple, but of the world....[7]

Yes, the world is the temple of Jesus. It is, at the very least, His exterior temple, for, in the deepest and truest sense, His temple and our temple is nothing but Himself. He is the Law, He is Tradition, He is the Covenant, He is the Temple. In many episodes, He designated Himself, He designated His body as the place which must be that of the presence of God for men, and that of adoration in spirit and in truth.[8] He who is the lord of the sabbath (Mt 12:8; Mk 2:28; Lk 6:5) is the lord of prayer. With a sovereign freedom, the freedom of the Lord, He frees prayer from the old forms and, first, the "consecrated" places: He who so much loved to pray in solitude invites His disciples to pray to the Father "in secret."[9]

[6] See Mt 4:23; 9:35; 13:54; Mk 1:21, 39; 6:2; Lk 4:15, 44; 6:6; Mt 26:55; Mk 12:35; 14:49; Lk 19:47; 20:1; 21:37; Jn 7:28; 8:20; 18:20.
[7] *Sermo 59 (De Passione 8),* c. 5: PL 54, 340; St. THOMAS AQUINAS quoting St. JOHN CHRYSOSTOM, *Summa Theologiae,* IIIa, q. 46, a. 10, ad 2.
[8] Cf. Jn 4:21–23, and see our *The Mystery of the Temple,* Westminster, 1962, pp. 117f.
[9] Mt 6:6; M. MEINERTZ, "Jesus und das Gebet," in *Die Kirche in der Welt,* 1 (1948), pp. 145–148.

The external framework for His prayer is, then, of little importance to Him. Nevertheless, Jesus was fond, for one thing, of solitude (cf. Lk 5:16; 9:18; Mt 14:23; 26:36 and parallel texts; Mk 1:35 and parallel texts; 6:46) and, for another, of the hills (Mt 14:23 [Mk 1:35]; Mk 6:46; Lk 6:12; 9:28). Without drifting into a sentimentality which is ruled out by the whole style of the Gospels and, especially, by the style of the prayers of Jesus which have been handed down to us, we must hold it as certain that Jesus, in order to erect the bridge of prayer towards His Father and provide Himself with favorable surroundings, had a great liking for the marvelously tonic solitude of places where a vast horizon stretches out, where the soul can feel withdrawn from the noises, the agitation, and the competition below.

It is difficult to single out the moments of Jesus' prayer, for prayer filled His whole life. Did not He Himself teach that we must pray without ceasing (Lk 18:1)? Busy all day long with spreading the Good News, even so busy that, as St. Mark says, Jesus and His disciples no longer had time to eat (6:31), our Master loved to pray at night, actually to spend nights in prayer.[10] Given the end pursued by the evangelists, we should not be surprised that they recounted many acts of the Lord's prayer in connection with His ministry.

Jesus opened His messianic ministry by being baptized by John: "When Jesus also had been baptized and was praying, the heaven was opened, and the Holy Spirit descended upon him in bodily form, as a dove, and a voice came from heaven, 'Thou art my beloved Son; with thee I am well pleased'" (Lk 3:21–22). This scene occurs once more during the transfiguration (Lk 9:28ff.), which is presented as an account of the consecration of Christ as minister of the new covenant, not of the letter,

---

[10] Lk 6:12; almost certainly Mt 14:23 and Mk 1:35; Gethsemani (Mk 22:14) is a special case.

but of the Spirit.[11] Jesus prayed before the choosing of the twelve (Lk 6:12), He prayed before He began preaching in Galilee, He prayed before Peter's confession of faith, He prayed especially for Peter (Lk 22:31). During His ministry, He laid His hands on others while praying (Mt 19:13). He who drove out so many unclean spirits said that this could not be done except by fasting and prayer (Mk 9:29). Many times, the development of His ministry or the accomplishment of the works of the Father drew forth from Him, like a cry, a prayer of thanksgiving (Mt 11:25; Lk 10:21; Jn 11:41).

But the supreme moment of the prayer of Jesus was the supreme moment of His ministry, the moment of His holy Passion, by which He established the new covenant in His blood and all the efficacy of the apostolic ministry. Three great acts are here interconnected: the Last Supper, the agony, the cross. The substance of them all was the same: it was love, it was the wholly filial obedience with which Jesus accomplished the will of His Father, even to His acceptance of death and His offering of that death for us, sinners, with whom God wished to preserve and renew forever His covenant of grace. It was on the cross that all was accomplished, but Jesus twice anticipated His sacrifice, as to its spiritual substance. He did this "on the night when He was handed over": once, in instituting its sacramental celebration and the corresponding ministry, in the upper room of the Cenacle; a second time, in revealing its real content, in the agony in the garden. These three acts of a single passion were filled with prayer. Jesus instituted the Eucharist during a celebration of the Pasch which called for a whole series of prayers and psalms. Jesus gave thanks;[12] He sang the psalms of the *Hallel* (cf. Mt

---

[11] 2 Cor 3:6. The passage contrasts the fading radiance of the face of Moses and the glory which illumines the face of Christ Jesus: cf. v. 18 and 4:6. St. THOMAS AQUINAS relates the scene of the Baptism to that of the Transfiguration: *I Sent.,* d. 16, q. 1, a. 3; *Summa Theologiae,* Ia, q. 43, a. 7.

[12] Mt 26:26f.; Mk 14:22f.; Lk 22:17, 19, 20.

26:30; Mk 4:26). He then pronounced, according to St. John, His great "priestly prayer," which we prefer to call His apostolic prayer, for He prays in it for His apostles, for the work of the apostolate, for the future of the community assembled by faith in His (and in their) word. This great prayer, which occupies the whole of the seventeenth chapter in St. John, is like the summation of Jesus's prayer. It brings together all the themes of the Our Father and of the other prayers reported to us in the Gospels. It is *the* prayer of Jesus going forth to His Father for our salvation.[13]

The agony was accompanied by a sublime prayer, whose crucial importance we will soon see. Finally, on the cross, Jesus prayed. He began, and undoubtedly finished right through to the end, Psalm 22: "My God, my God, why hast thou forsaken me?", which closes with the certainty of an invincible hope (cf. Mt 27:46; Mk 15:34). He gave up the spirit while repeating another verse from the Psalms: "Father, into thy hands I commit my spirit" (Lk 23:46; Ps 31:6).

The Our Father Sums Up All the Prayer of Christ

The style of the prayer of Jesus is revealed in the prayers to which we have just alluded and, with the most unimpeachable authenticity, in the *Pater*. We find nothing sentimental in it, no bombast, no rhetoric. With God also, our word must be "Yes? Yes. No? No" (Mt 5:37). We must not be forever repeating the same old thing, as the pagans do (cf. Mt. 6:17). The prayer of Jesus is simple and manly, direct, sure, filled with nobility and grandeur. It translates in perfect fashion the filial attitude, made up of submission and love, confidence and fearlessness, of which Jesus is the very revelation.

Scripture is not very specific about the concrete aspects, external and perceptible, of the prayer of Jesus. He raised His eyes

[13] See A. GEORGE, *art. cit., supra,* note 4.

to heaven (cf. Mk 7:34; Jn 11:41; 17:1). During His agony, He prayed on His knees (Lk 22:41) and even prostrated with His face to the ground (Mt 26:39). He prayed with loud cries and tears (cf. Heb 5:7). Outside of these particular instances, Scripture says nothing about the bodily attitudes Jesus preferred while praying. Did He stand up? Did He bend His knees, as in Christian practice?[14] This is not made clear.

The prayer of Jesus embraces the two great themes of all prayer: simple praise and petition. The *Pater* itself is thus apportioned. It sums up all the prayer of Jesus, all Christian prayer, and we understand why the Christian authors who wanted to write a treatise on prayer simply commented on the Our Father. This apportionment into two parts evidently corresponds to the double and unique commandment of love of God and of our neighbor, and also to the two tables of the Law which are summed up and consummated in this love.

We have heard Jesus giving thanks (Mt 11:25; Lk 10:21; Jn 11:41; and note 12 above). Jesus loved His Father so much and adhered to His will with so much filial love that He experienced, in the Holy Spirit, great thrills of joy in seeing the Father's design of salvation being realized, a design which was to lead to glory, not by the way of exaltation and power, but by the way of abasement and weakness.[15] It cannot be questioned that this prayer of loving and joyous adherence to the will of the Father was coextensive with the whole earthly life of Jesus, so much so that, against the demon, against the general opinion which thought of the Messiah as a triumphant warrior, against the worldly understanding of His own kin and, until the very last day, the worldly understanding of His own disciples, Jesus

---

[14] Cf. Eph 3:14; Acts 20:36; 21:5.

[15] Lk 10:21; Mt 11:25 and many passages where Jesus recognizes that God's plan is to be accomplished through the cross, adheres to this plan, then explains it to His disciples (Lk 24:35f., 44f.). Cf. 1 Cor 1:26–29; Phil 2:5–11; Heb 2:10–13; 5:8; 12:2.

had to reaffirm unceasingly the plan of salvation by the cross and to define His own role in this plan.

We have also seen that Jesus liked to pray solely for the sake of praying, simply to express His communion with His Father, to hallow His Name. For Him, there was no separation, hardly even a difference of detail, between adoration and adherence to the plan of God. It is generally recognized that the first three formulas of the Our Father are equivalent to one another: the name is hallowed when the Kingdom comes, when the will of God is done on earth as it is in heaven. There can be no doubt that these three prayers filled the hours and the nights of adoration which Jesus so often spent in loving adherence to His Father and the praise of His glory. From His Son, who had taken our flesh, the Father drew a perfect praise. . . .[16]

Theology tells us that the prayer of petition follows upon hope, of which it is only a translation. What could Christ hope for, for what could He petition? The guidance of the Gospel allows us to specify the objects of His petition. For Himself, Jesus asked for His own glorification, and this at the moment when He was entering upon His passion: Jn 17:1 and 5. His glorification is, in the first place, a matter of His resurrection. Jesus, who shuddered at and was profoundly troubled by the prospect of His ignominious death (Mt 26:37-38; Mk 14:33-34), Jesus who wished to be saved from this hour (Jn 12:27), prayed at that very moment that His Father glorify His name in Him. During His agony, He offered up prayers and supplications, with loud cries and tears, to Him who was able to save Him from death (Heb 5:7)—not by sparing Him from it, but by giving

16 The old Dominican Breviary included an Office of "The Finding of our Lord Jesus Christ in the Midst of the Teachers" (Sunday within the Octave of the Epiphany), in which the contemplative and praying soul of Christ shone forth. The antiphon for the first psalm of Matins was: "*Elevata est magnificentia tua, Deus, super coelos, qui ex ore Filii tui perfecisti laudem.*"

Him life beyond that death, as He had already done for Isaac, He, the God of the living![17] Indeed, with His resurrection and beyond it, the glorification of Jesus embraces the full execution of the last chapter of the plan of God as it pertains to Him: His resurrection, His heavenly exaltation, His power as Lord being applied to communicate eternal life, the sending of the Holy Spirit, the whole of His active presence in His own and in His Church. By means of them all, He, once glorified, will achieve the glorification of the Father which He began by realizing to the letter the beginning of the program, marked with the sign of the cross.[18]

Jesus prayed before choosing the apostles (Lk 6:12), He prayed before the confession of Peter (Lk 9:18), and He prayed that Peter's faith might not fail (Lk 22:32). When St. Matthew (14:23) and St. Mark (6:46) tell us that Jesus withdrew into the hills, in solitude, to pray, they are leading up to the account of the occasion when the apostles' boat was buffeted by a great tempest which only the coming of the Master would allay. Jesus prayed then for the apostles, He prayed for the Church. He asked for them, for it, the sending of another Counselor (Jn 14:16). Finally, His supreme prayer, in which all the prayer of His life was summed up, was for the disciples, for those whom the Father had given Him: that the Father watch over them, that they be one, that they have in them the fullness of joy, that they be consecrated in truth. Jesus did not pray only for them, but for all those who, by their words, would believe in Him, so that all might be one (Jn 17). This unity is one which is drawn from the unity of the divine Persons and is an image of theirs. Jesus

---

[17] Cf. Rom 4:18–21; Heb 11:17–19; Mt 22:32.
[18] Jesus does not seek *His* glory: Jn 7:18; 8:50, but that of His Father, which is, of course, inseparable from His own: Jn 12:28; 13:31; 17:24. On the glory of the Son, see A. M. RAMSEY, *The Glory of God and the Transfiguration of Christ,* London, 1949.

did not give all the implications in detail, but it is quite certain that these were, and still are, the object of His intercession, for He does not cease to make intercession for us.[19] The field is unbounded, covering the entire history of salvation. This is a history in which the few years of life given to each are such a little thing, yet something very precious, something absolutely unique. Jesus embraced all this and He embraces all in His prayer. How immense this is, and how profound!

The objects of Jesus' petition are well-defined: His own exaltation and His Church, which is His body. An early author wrote: "All His life long, He prayed to the Father for the resurrection of His body and for our salvation."[20] These objects correspond exactly to what He could hope for; the prayer of Christ, in what He asks for, exactly corresponds to His hope. The existence of some kind of hope in the soul of Christ is not to be questioned. All that theologians discuss is its exact nature and the way it is to be fitted into the organism of virtues, as they conceive and define them. We leave to one side this problem of conceptualization,[21] and limit our consideration to the concrete reality of a real

[19] Cf. Rom 8:34; Heb 7:25; 8:6; 9:24; 1 Jn 2:1. Compare 1 Jn 2:14, 16.

[20] Hervé DE BOURG-DIEU (twelfth century), *Ennarr. in epist. ad Hebr.,* c. 5 (*PL* 181, 1566C), a text sometimes wrongly attributed to Anselm of Laon, and even to St. Anselm.

[21] The solution given to the problem of Christ's hope during His earthly life depends on one's idea of the vision of God which He enjoyed. Classical theology makes no distinction between that vision and the vision of heavenly, eschatological beatitude. But E. GUTWENGER, S.J. (*Bewusstein und Wissen Christi. Eine dogmatische Studie,* Innsbruck, 1960, pp. 131f., 153f.) proposes the attribution to Christ of an immediate vision of God, though not one which is beatifying in the sense of the fullness of heavenly joy and glory; and this because of the salvific economy which made of Christ a Saviour by the cross, subject to the infirmities which this role demanded. Gutwenger thus explains certain "ignorances" in Christ, particularly His ignorance of the day of judgment. St. THOMAS AQUINAS, as is known, denied the existence in Christ of a theological hope, properly speaking: IIIa, q. 7, a. 4: *Quaest. disp. de Spe,* a. 4, ad 16. While hope is, on the one hand, considered by St. Thomas as formally applicable only to what one hopes for himself, *theological* hope, on the other hand, is that hope by

THE PRAYER OF CHRIST

hope, in Jesus, not only of what He expected from God during
the days of His passable flesh, but also of what He expected from
Him for His body, which is the Church, and for the salvation
of the world. It would be helpful to reread in this connection
the splendid text in which Origen comments, conjointly, on Mk
14:25 (Mt 26:29; Lk 22:18): "I shall not drink again of the
fruit of the vine until that day when I drink it new in the kingdom of God" and 1 Cor 15:28: "When all things are subjected
to him, then the Son himself will also be subjected to him who
put all things under him, that God may be everything to every
one." Origen shows that something is lacking to Christ, something is lacking to the joy of Christ, to such an extent that all, in
each and in all, is not completely subjected to the Father. We
cannot separate His members from Christ. As long as there is

which one hopes to obtain the possession of *God* Himself—and Christ possessed God. One would then speak, in regard to Christ, of a hope in the
ordinary sense of the word, something which would be called, rather, "trust"
and would be theologically analyzed under either the passion of hope, or
moral hope, or confidence, with its source in the virtue of fortitude. As for
the desire for our beatitude or the completion of His mystical body, there
would be hope only in an improper sense, really related to charity: thus the
Thomists, J. M. RAMIREZ, O.P. ("De spei Christianae fideique divinae
dependentia," in *Divus Thomas*, Fribourg, 1940, pp. 211–284; cf. pp. 225,
233–235); Charles JOURNET, *L'Eglise du Verbe incarné*, vol. II, Paris, 1951,
pp. 154f. Various points in this Thomistic interpretation can be questioned,
and have in fact been questioned: the place given to the resurrection,
"beatitude of body" treated as accidental with regard to beatitude; the idea
that one can formally hope only for himself. Pierre CHARLES, S.J., cites on
this subject St. THOMAS AQUINAS himself, IIa-IIae, q. 17, a. 3: "*Praesup-
posita unione amoris ad alterum, jam aliquis potest sperare et desiderare
alteri vitam aeternam, in quantum est ei unitus per amorem*": "Spes Christi,"
in *NRT*, 1934, pp. 1009–1021 (reprinted in *L'Eglise, sacrement du monde*,
Paris-Bruges, 1960, pp. 74–83). Père Charles thinks that it is impossible to
consider Christian hope in a totally personal-individual fashion; the members of Christ's body cannot be separated from Christ; consequently, he
speaks of a hope in Christ, even in heaven, whose object is to obtain from
God salvation or beatitude for all those whose Saviour and mediator He is.
Père DE LUBAC has put forward the same idea (*Catholicism*, New York,
1950, pp. 53f.), citing, to this effect, some fine texts from Origen and St.
Gregory of Nyssa (cf. note following); Père BROUTIN has done the same,
Mysterium Ecclesiae, Paris, 1945, pp. 243–249.

97

something to obtain for us, to hope for for us, there remains, in Christ, a hope and a prayer. . . .[22]

Prayer, Communion in the Mystery and in the Will of God

Let us attempt an overall view of the prayer of Jesus, under the aspect of its substance; let us attempt to understand how it is bound up with a single root of prayer which was the very root of His life and in which His adoration, His petition, and His thanksgiving were united. There does, in fact, exist an essential prayer, simple and total, which exceeds and embraces all particular prayers. In it, such prayers are germinated in the measure that the truth of our religious attitude calls them forth.

All prayer is communion in the mystery and in the will of God. This essential prayer consists in being receptive and wholly offered to God so that He might be God, not only in Himself— for He is always this; He is this no less without us than with us—but also in His creation: in us, in others, and in the world.[23] He is always God in Himself: to His consubstantial glory men can neither add nor take anything away. But God wishes to radiate His glory for the benefit of creatures whom He freely calls into existence, and to diffuse in them a reflection of His own life: His truth, His justice, His love. . . . To pray is to be in communion in joy, in submission, is thanksgiving, with this mystery of God in Himself and in us, to be in communion with the unique Source and to offer oneself. We make this offering as much to receive what the Source destines for us, in the spirit of finding His joy in what He has given us to be, to have and to

---

[22] ORIGEN, *Hom. 7 in Levit.*, 2 (*PG* 12, 478–482; Baehrens edition, pp. 374–380); ET in H. DE LUBAC, *op. cit.*, pp. 235–240, which is followed by a text, pp. 240–241, from St. GREGORY OF NYSSA, *Treatise on the text: "Then the Son himself shall be subject "* (*PG* 44, 1316–1321).

[23] Compare the prayer of St. CATHERINE OF SIENA: "Mercy to Catherine! Mercy to the Church! Mercy to the world!"

98

do (cf. Jn 3:27–30), as to make of ourselves, if God wills it, the channel of what He destines for others, and even for the whole world. To pray is to be in communion with the mystery and with the will of God, to be in communion with His glory, in Himself and in His creation, by means of the radiation of which we have spoken, in virtue of which the glory of God and the life of men coincide.[24] The themes of the *Pater* have no other content. The name of the Father is hallowed when His Kingdom comes: not a kingdom of pure domination, in the fashion of a tyrant, but a kingdom which communicates all His goods and makes us reign with Him when we do His will on earth as in heaven. To pray is, then, to say, not only with one's lips, but with all one's heart and with the most profound dispositions: "You are my God," in all the circumstances in which we find ourselves: our joy, our trials, our undertakings, our solitude, our human relationships, our health, our illness, and, finally, our death. . . . "You are my God; you will always be my God. I want you to be God for me and in me, for all men and in all men, for the world and all that is in it."

This, basically, is the prayer of the Psalms. It is the prayer of the people of God saying: "You are God! May you be God! You are my God, you will always be my God!", in all the circumstances of defeat and of well-being, of danger and of gladness, of simple joy in the service of God, of penitence and supplication, that this people knew. It is the prayer of Israel expressing its fidelity and singing it to the God of the covenant. The Psalms are as well the prayer of every soul which remains faithful in all the vicissitudes of life. They are the prayer of petition, and even of supplication, body for militant body (cf. Col 4:12), they are the prayer of imprecation directed against the Evil One and those who, along with him, resist the Gospel,

---

[24] Cf. St. IRENAEUS: *"Gloria Dei vivens homo; vita hominis, visio Dei"* (*Adversus Haereses,* IV, 20, 7: *PG* 7, 1037).

the prayer of the praise of the power of God who triumphs over evil and death, the prayer, finally, of thanksgiving for all! We are sure that Jesus prayed the prayer of the Psalms. The Gospels, indeed, vouch for this once or twice, but, well beyond such testimony, there is the fact that the incarnate Word assumed a Jewish humanity, a religious humanity as well. He first prayed the prayer of the people of God. The Letter to the Hebrews makes no mistake when, wishing to express the intention and the sentiments of Jesus in His incarnation, it borrows the text of a psalm which sums up the entire movement of revelation in regard to the worship of God: "Sacrifices and offerings thou hast not desired, but a body hast thou prepared for me; in burnt offerings and sin offerings thou hast taken no pleasure. Then I said, 'Lo, I have come to do thy will, O God'" (Ps 40:7–8, in the version of the Septuagint; Heb 10:5–7).

Jesus, Center and Summit of Universal Prayer

Yes, Jesus sums up, assumes and consummates, in His prayer, all the prayer of the people of God. Still more, the prayer of the whole world.

Abraham was magnificently receptive and wholly offered so that, in him and by him, God might act as God, that He might effect in him and by him His design of covenant. Moses too was wonderfully receptive and wholly offered, and, after him, David, Elijah, the prophets, the countless faithful Jews who went up to the Temple to pray, according to the law of the covenant, so very many "poor of Yahweh" who were awaiting the consolation of Israel. . . . John the Baptist was heroically receptive and wholly offered to the will of God which was coming to visit His people. How great indeed, in a prayer totally submissive and stripped of self-seeking, was his adherence to the plan of salvation and of covenant whose imminent realization he was charged to announce to the world! And the Virgin Mary, through whom

100

he Source Himself would burst upon the world! How receptive
ınd how wholly offered she was in the adoration, submission, and
thanksgiving of her prayer, so that through her there might be
ealized in its fullness the mercy promised to Abraham and to
ıis posterity forever! (Lk 1:38, 54–55).

In His own prayer, Jesus gathered together, summed up, and
:onsummated all these prayers which were leading to Him. He
s the whole of the promises, He is the absolute Yes of the divine
ıhilanthropy and of God's design of salvation for the entire
vorld.[25] When Jesus, in entering the world, says: "Sacrifices and
ıfferings thou hast not desired, but a body hast thou prepared
or me. . . . Then I said, 'Lo, I have come to do thy will, O God,' "
Ie not only epitomizes the substance of His own prayer, but
Ie also carries on and consummates thereby everything that was
nsufficient in all the prayers and all the sacrifices offered before
Iim. He is the all of faithful prayer.

He is the all of the prayer of the world. From the day when
the Second Person of the Holy Trinity took flesh in the womb
ıf Mary, there began to beat in the world a perfectly filial heart;
there existed a human consciousness and freedom which were
·eceptive and wholly offered to God so that His will of salvation
:ould be perfectly unfolded. The world had found its center or
ıummit of prayer of adoration, of entreaty, of communion in
the mystery of God, and of thanksgiving. It is not simply the
ırayer of faithful souls, but also the groaning in travail of all
:reation, waiting for a total redemption (cf. Rom 8:18–25),
which pass through the consciousness and prayer of Him who
s the First-born of every creature, the Principle, the First-born
from the dead (Col 1:15 and 18; Heb 1:6). "*Per Dominum
Nostrum Jesum Christum*": everything passes through Him. He
is the unique Priest, the world's great celebrant.

Adoration, petition, or thanksgiving, His prayer is addressed

[25] Cf. 2 Cor 1:20; Tit 3:4; Jn 11:52.

101

to the Father. The prayers whose wording has been handed on to us by the Gospels open with an invocation to the Father.[26] It was under this title that He taught us to address God: "Our Father." As He Himself prays in us by His Spirit, the Spirit which makes us cry *Abba!* Father! (Rom 8:15, 26–27), Jesus Himself is somehow involved with us in the "our" of the *Pater;* it is truly our common Father whom He taught us to invoke. He did, however, hint at a distinction by saying: "my Father and your Father, my God and your God" (Jn 20:17). He is the same and not the same. It is as man that Jesus prays to God, and so, in a certain fashion, He is at our level, but only in a certain fashion. Even when He prays as man, He whom He invokes is, by an absolutely unique and divine title, the Father of the holy Person to whom this human prayer belongs, the Father in the absolute sense of the divine trinitarian ontology. The fact that this "Father of our Lord Jesus Christ" has been given to us by grace, but truly as Father, permits us to use, when addressing Him, the invocation of the Lord Jesus, but it does not abolish the distinction.

St. Augustine often went back to the prayer of Christ. He liked to expand upon a triple reflection which we find in rather typical fashion in his commentary on Psalm 85 (Heb. 86). He views Christ under three aspects: as our priest or mediator, He prays for us; as having taken human flesh, He is the head of a body of which we form the members, thus constituting with Him a single perfect man: He prays in us; as God, considered in His condition of God, *in forma Dei,* He is prayed by us.

Let us begin with this third aspect. From the apostolic origins of the Church, Christ was prayed as God or Lord: see 2 Cor 12:8; 1 Tim 1:12. Towards the years 111–113, Pliny the Younger, making a report to the emperor Trajan, tells us that Christians ad-

[26] See Mt 6:9; 11:25, 26; Mk 14:36; Lk 23:34, 46. Compare Jn 17:1, 5, 21, 24, 25; 11:41; 12:27–28.

dressed hymns to Christ as to God.[27] This is not the place to write a history of the worship rendered to Christ nor of the prayer addressed to Jesus as Lord: there are numerous monographs on the subject. The Church followed this tradition, and followed it with all the more fervor and application as she was forced, for centuries, to oppose the Arian heresy and its sequels among the barbarous peoples who settled in the West from the fifth century onwards. We adore Christ, we pray to Him, we give Him thanks (cf. the *Gloria in excelsis*).

The New Testament tells us that Christ intercedes for us as our priest (cf. note 19). This is especially true of the Letter to the Hebrews, which tells us again and again that we have in Him a great high priest who sympathizes with us (4:14–15; 10:10, 19ff.), who is able to make intercession for us and to save us (7:25; 9:25). He was, by His blood, the mediator of a new covenant (9:15; 12:24; 13:20); through Him, we offer up to God a sacrifice of praise (13:15; cf. 1 Pet 2:5). Thus Christ is, as Clement of Alexandria expressed it, "the peaceful instrument through whom we praise the Father."[28] We pray only through Him, as the liturgy habitually has us say: "*Per Dominum nostrum. . . .*" We thus offer to the Father our most sacred title to be heard by Him.

The Fathers of the Church, St. Augustine in particular, liked to see in the verse from the discussion with Nicodemus, "No one has ascended into heaven but he who descended from heaven, the Son of man who is in heaven" (Jn 3:13), an allusion to the reality of the mystical body. Truly, there is but one Son, one sole heir of God: we are sons only in the Son, heirs only in the Heir.[29]

[27] *Epist. liber.*, 10, 96, n. 7 (KIRCH, *Enchiridion Fontium Historiae ecclesiasticae antiquae*, Freiburg, 1923, no. 30).
[28] *Paedagogus*, II, 4 (*PG* 8, 441B).
[29] Cf. Rom 8:17; Gal 3:26; 4:6, and the entire theme of Christ-as-New Adam (Rom 5:12f.; 1 Cor 15); E. MERSCH, "*Filii in Filio*," Chapter 12, *The Theology of the Mystical Body*, St. Louis, 1952.

We have existence before God only *in Jesus Christ*. This is not by the simple plan of faith, which makes us live a life to the account of Christ and would then credit the merits of justice—the justice of Christ—to my own account. It is by the reality of a life communicated from Christ, one which makes us depend on Him as the cells of a body depend on the vital principle of the whole organism, which appears to be connected with the head. We know how the scholastics of the twelfth and thirteenth centuries elaborated a theology of Christ-as-Head. According to St. Thomas Aquinas in particular, all grace passes through Christ, not as through an inanimate instrument, but as through a living and conscious one, intelligent and free. It is through the consciousness of Christ, through the knowledge of His intellect, through the love of His heart and the free decision of His will, that the realization of the whole merciful design of God passes. We receive no spiritual gift which has not been willed for us by Christ, who knows us and who loves us. What we said above about the prayer of Christ thus takes on all its value. When Jesus, in His prayer, was receptive and wholly offered, as to His consciousness, His freedom, His life, so that God might realize through Him His whole design of salvation, He brought His will into harmony with that of the Father. He embraced us in this prayer; it was in our regard that He, in some way, was acting.

By this efficacious action, Christ conforms us and incorporates us into Himself. Lacking existence before God except through Him, we live truly by Him and, no less, in Him. We become the unique reality, made up nonetheless of individual persons and individual freedoms, which is the communional body or, as has been said since the middle of the twelfth century, the "mystical body" of Christ. A single filial being, who says "*Pater Noster*," is constituted, a single being of love, a single adorer, a single prayer. This is why St. Augustine, once again developing the commentary on Jn 3:13 which we mentioned above, interprets in this sense the passage of the Gospel which shows Jesus

104

THE PRAYER OF CHRIST

as going up the mountain to pray *alone* (Mt 14:23). "The mountain," he says, "represents height. What is there in the world which is higher than heaven? Now you, the faithful, know prefectly well *who* it was who ascended to heaven: 'No one has ascended into heaven but he who descended from heaven, the Son of man who is in heaven.' Although He must come at the end and then assemble us all as His own members to raise us to heaven, even then He will go up alone, because the head with its body forms one single Christ."

We know that this idea or, what amounts to the same thing, the doctrine of the mystical body of Christ, formed the basis of the theology of the liturgy proposed by Pius XII in the encyclical *Mediator Dei* (November 20th, 1947). The liturgy is a privileged activity of prayer. It is not so much the faithful dialogue of the Church and her Lord as it is the voice of the bride and the voice of the Bridegroom *united* to praise the Father—especially in the Eucharistic prayer, which is the universal thanksgiving *of Christ* taken up and pronounced by the Church. The prayer which is celebrated in the Eucharist is unconditionally the prayer of Christ and, in a very special way, it is *this* prayer, addressed to God by Christ in His passion and, in the Letter to the Hebrews, attributed to Christ as the precise purpose for which He came into the world: Yes, Father! Amen to your will!

When our personal prayer is in question, everything depends on our union with Christ and also on the authenticity of our prayer in taking up the line of His own, that is to say, in being receptive and wholly offered so that in us, through us, in and through Christ, God might accomplish His design and might manifest His glory. In the measure in which we live in Him, and He in us, Christ prays with us, prays in us. St. Paul ascribes this intimate presence and activity to the Holy Spirit, but He is the Spirit *of the Son,* and that is why He cries *Abba!* Father! (Rom 8:15; Gal 4:6). It is through the Spirit of Jesus Christ, it is in

Jesus Christ—and He in us—that we say "Our Father." When we ask, then, for our daily bread, we are certainly asking for bread for ourselves, and even for our material support, but also for the bread of Christ in humanity and for the bread of men "in Christ"; we are asking for the bread of the mystical body for this today of grace. It is also in union with Jesus Christ that we take up that other "Lord's Prayer" which is the prayer for unity, in St. John, Chapter 17: "Father, that they may be one as we are one. . . ." The extraordinary power of purifying, of strengthening, and of pacifying, the almost sacramental fruitfulness of this prayer for unity, unquestionably stem from the fact that it was prayed, that it is always prayed by Jesus, and that it is He who prays it in us.

4

The Preaching of Christ

The Parables, Revelatory of the God Who Is to Come

A MISSIONARY pedagogy. —The parables, revelation of the Kingdom of God. —The parables, revelation of the "heart" of man. —The parables in the economy of salvation.

A Missionary Pedagogy

"Why do you speak to them in parables?"

The Gospel began in Galilee. Even if Jesus, immediately afterwards, interrupted His Galilean ministry by several trips to Jerusalem, as we learn from the fourth Gospel, Jesus preached for a long while principally in Galilee. He preached by using parables. The first three Gospels, in an almost brutal way, have made this plain. We can easily be disturbed by this, especially if, while failing to take into account the limited resources of the Hebrew language, we interpret the text of Isaiah used by our Lord in the sense of an active and formal intention, on the part of God, to make blind and to harden the hearers of His message.[1]

[1] Père CONDAMIN (*Le Livre d'Isaïe*, pp. 45–46) writes on the subject of Is 6:9f.: "We must take Semitic language and thought into account. . . . Between the *causative* sense and the *permissive* sense, there is an intermediate sense, of which we have an example here: *to give occasion* to the action expressed by the verb. The preaching of Isaiah, owing to the poor dis-

Let us cite here the texts of St. Matthew and St. Mark; Lk 8:9–10 gives an abridged version, and Jn 12:37–40 makes the evangelical witness on this point unanimous.[2]

Mt 13:10–15	Mk 4:10–12 and 33–34
Then the disciples came and said to him, "Why do you speak to them in parables?" And he answered them, "To you it has been given to know the secrets of the kingdom of heaven, but to them it has not been given. For to him who has will more be given, and he will have abundance; but from him who has not, even what he has will be taken away. This is why I speak to them in parables, because seeing they do not see, and hearing they do not hear, nor do they understand. With them indeed is ful-	And when he was alone, those who were about him with the twelve asked him concerning the parables. And he said to them, "To you has been given the secret of the kingdom of God, but for those outside everything is in parables; so that *they may indeed see but not perceive, and may indeed hear but not understand; lest they should turn again, and be forgiven.*" . . . With many such parables he spoke the word to them, as they were able to hear it; he did not speak to them without a parable, but privately to his

positions of his hearers, will be the *occasion* of their callousness. Finally, we must reckon with the Semitic approach to things, considering secondary causes hardly at all and readily referring every event to God, first and principal cause. This approach is well served by the language which distinguishes poorly between the various kinds of causality; when God *permits* what He foresees and could prevent, He is deemed to *do: He hardens* the heart of Pharaoh, etc." Cf. J. BUZY, *Introduction aux Paraboles évangéliques*, Paris, 1912, pp. 333f; L. DE GRANDMAISON, *Jesus Christ. His Person, His Message, His Credentials*, London, 1932, vol. II, pp. 34f.; J. GUITTON, *Portrait de Monsieur Pouget*, Paris, 1940, p. 111 (ET *Abbé Pouget Discourses*, Baltimore, 1959).

2 The reference to Is 6:9f. is thus certified as going back to our Lord Himself. It was a *"topos"* of the apostolic preaching, then a piece in the collections of biblical texts (*testimonia*) used by the Christians to show that the unbelief of the Jews had been foretold. Cf. Acts 28:24–27 (cf. Rom 11:7–9; 2 Cor 3:14–15); L. CERFAUX, "'L'aveuglement d'esprit' dans l'Evangile de saint Marc," in *Le Muséon*, 59 (1946), pp. 267–279 (reprinted in *Recueil Lucien Cerfaux*, Gembloux, 1954, vol. II, pp. 3–15). According to the text of Isaiah followed, this process of obscuring is more or less connected with the intention of God; St. Matthew's style of quotation does so more, St. Mark's less.

THE PREACHING OF CHRIST

filled the prophecy of Isaiah which says: '*You shall indeed hear but never understand, and you shall indeed see but never perceive. For this people's heart has grown dull, and their ears are heavy of hearing, and their eyes they have closed, lest they should perceive with their eyes, and hear with their ears, and understand with their heart, and turn for me to heal them.*' "

own disciples he explained everything.

We shall retain the distinction made by Jesus—later on, we shall see more of it—between the *disciples,* who have already committed themselves to Him and who "believe," at least in principle, and the *hearers* to whom Jesus addresses Himself, possibly for the first time, with a view to leading them to hear the Good News of the Kingdom and to adhere to it. To the latter, Jesus proposes His message in parables, in such a way that they can hear and not hear.

Attempts have been made to explain in different ways this sort of tactic, which seems surprising at first.[3] It has been sometimes seen as a punishment, a sanction which was merited by the pride and insubordination of the Jews; sometimes, more often in fact—and with better reason, besides—it has been seen as an act of mercy: Jesus wished to teach His hearers as they could be taught, in a way which would considerately engage their responsibility without making it too much worse. There are, though, a number of authors who, when all is said and done,

---

[3] The principal monographs, besides that of BUZY, cited in note 1, are: F. LA CAVA, "*Ut videntes non videant.*" *Il motivo e lo scopo delle parabole nel Vangelo,* Rome, 1934; C. H. DODD, *The Parables of the Kingdom,* London, 1935 (4th ed., 1938); M. HERMANIUK, *La Parabole évangélique. Enquête exégétique et critique,* Bruges-Paris, 1947; A. DENZER, *The Parables of the Kingdom . . . ,* Washington, 1945 (classification of opinions; thesis of mercy); L. DE GRANDMAISON, *op. et loc. cit.* —A recent study on "the messianic secret" is Erik SJOLLBERG, *Der verborgene Menschensohn in den Evangelien,* Lund, 1955 (cf. *RechScRel,* 1958, pp. 260f.).

merge the two explanations. The Jews to whom Jesus was speaking had in mind a somewhat earthly, warlike and quite triumphalist conception of the messianic king. Jesus could not offer Himself to them as Messiah without running the risk of provoking reactions of rather impure enthusiasm, which would be far removed from faith in the Servant-through-the-cross which He had to be (cf. Mt 12:15–19). Furthermore, to present Himself at the very start as the suffering Servant would be to strike so hard at the mentality of His hearers as to have the effect of closing their minds forever. At all events, it was necessary not to precipitate the conclusion: the preaching of the Gospel called for a "period of grace" which Jesus could bring about by a preaching which was clear enough so that one could hear and be converted to the Gospel, allusive and discreet enough so that one would not be faced all of a sudden with a truth he was incapable of understanding. The ways of the Lord are, as ever, justice and mercy. To minds which brought with them so much slowness, so much hesitancy, even aversion, in receiving His word, Jesus uncovered a light which they more than half refused; but at the same time He showed them also something of this light, and He kept half-open for them the possibility of coming to it and recognizing it. The parabolical style brought into play by Him, from then on, corresponded to this purpose and, somewhow or other, to this "economy." It is a particular mode of revelation, or of manifestation of the mystery of God and His Kingdom. Putting aside any technical discussion, we would like to explain this mode by showing in the parables first a power to reveal the Kingdom, then a power to reveal hearts.

The Parables, Revelation of the Kingdom of God

"The Kingdom of Heaven is like . . ."

We are less concerned here with the parabolic genre or method as such than with the *content* of the parables. However diverse they may be, they are strikingly homogeneous in what they objectively express or suggest. Like all of Scripture, they speak to us of God and of ourselves; their aim is to make us understand the true rapport which must be established between the two, a rapport based on what God is for us and what He asks us to be for Him.

God is revealed less in Himself than as man's partner, a sovereign partner, to be sure, with the initiative and with the last word. He is rarely characterized in Himself, independently of what He does for us. He appears above all as the active term in everything that concerns man or is asked of him. This is no less true of the Gospel of John the Theologian, which sets before us a revelation of the intimate mystery of God. Even though St. John's Gospel contains no parables (the discourse on the Good Shepherd is almost the only one, and it is hardly a parable at all), the fourth Gospel brings the parabolic genre very much into action, but in another fashion and without recording any parables, properly speaking. In St. John, we have a teaching by means of enigmatic statements, in which there is something more to be understood, something beyond the words or actions taken materially. . . .[4] In the first three Gospels, on the other hand, and in St. Matthew especially, there are a good many parables. To a greater extent, they continue in the line of revelation of the Old Testament, through which God revealed less what He is in Himself than what He asks us to be for Him. A contemporary Jewish author, Abraham Heschel, was able to write: "The Bible is not a theology for man, but an anthropology for God." It uncovers for us the truth of the religious rapport by setting forth all sorts of concrete situations which present man as living out this rapport, sometimes well, sometimes badly, and

[4] See L. CERFAUX, Le Thème parabolique dans l'Evangile de Saint Jean: Conjectanea Neotestamentica, XI (in honor of A. Fridrichsen), Lund, 1948, pp. 15–25 (reprinted in Recueil Lucien Cerfaux, vol. II, pp. 17–26).

which envision and present God more as the sovereign term of this rapport.

Man is portrayed first as an object of mercy, and God, correlatively, as concerned about men who are going astray: He goes off in search of the lost sheep (Mt 18:12–14; Lk 15:4–7). St. Luke includes this parable, and adds to it not only the one about the lost coin, but also the unforgettable parable of the prodigal son: "There was a man who had two sons. . . ." God is a father, who reserves a special treatment for the son whom He had been in danger of losing (Lk 15:11–32). "The Son of man came to seek and to save the lost" (Lk 19:10).

Man is then shown to us as *called,* and even as *invited.* He is called to the Kingdom of God, which is essentially a banquet where all is in readiness, and we are the invited guests (Mt 22:1ff.; Lk 14:16ff.). We are not invited because of our qualities: the ones who are most qualified often fail to answer and the ones called in their place to fill the banquet room are the crippled and the left-behinds—one who was lost and is found again brings more joy than the ninety-nine others who had never left the fold.

A distinct break and a firm step forward are required. When confronted by the call to the Kingdom of God, we must make a choice. The parables of the Kingdom present this choice to us as one which involves letting go of something, indeed leaving all, for a single asset which is preferable to all others: the treasure found hidden in a field, the pearl of great value, the marriage feast (cf. Mt 13:44ff.; 22:1ff.). We must take hold of the opportunity presented, and this means making up our minds, accepting the inconveniences, getting into action. . . . When such an offer is made to us, such an invitation addressed, a variety of responses is possible, as the Lord's parable of the sower reveals to us (Mt 13:3ff.; Mk 4:3–20; Lk 8:5ff.). Some men are inattentive, are, as it were, oblivious to their unfathomable destiny, and these men offer the Word as much chance of penetrating as

112

an asphalt road offers to a seed which falls upon it and is eagerly picked up by the neighboring birds; other men, superficial, and lacking in spiritual loam, show an initial good will but it lacks any likelihood of a solid tomorrow: the Word puts forth no roots which would make it possible for it to resist the assault of trials; still other men try to forget and allow to be stifled the germ of a higher life which they have received but which will never have a future. There are also those who let themselves be penetrated by the Word, who nourish it with their lives while letting their lives be nourished by it, and in whom it bears fruit with greater or lesser abundance.

The parable of the sower does not develop the postulate of total refusal, but there are others which do: the two sons (Mt 21:28ff.), the murderous vine-dressers, a parable which is directed at the official elites of the Jewish people (Mt 21:33–41; Mk 12:1ff.; Lk 20:9ff.). Other parables illustrate the duty of watchfulness and availability: we must be ready like the steward whose master can return at any moment (Mt 24:45–51; Lk 12:42–48), like the maidens awaiting the wedding party (Mt 25:1–13; Lk 12:35–40): "Watch, therefore, for you know neither the day nor the hour." . . .

An initial welcome will not be enough: its earnestness must be established. In this area, words are of little weight, it is deeds that are called for: "The action is worth more than the sermon" (Claudel). There is probably no parable which expresses this better, and probably no parable which is more consoling for generous but disgruntled souls, than the parable of the two sons who were sent by their father to work in the vineyard: the first says, "I go, sir," and doesn't move a muscle; the second grumbles and says "no," but goes after all (Mt 21:28ff.). Jesus concludes: "The tax collectors and the harlots go into the kingdom of God before you. . . ." There are more who are called than are chosen. To have answered "yes" is not enough, nor is it enough to have made some effort and to have come to the banquet: we must

113

be wearing our wedding garment (Mt 22:11–14). God calls us to His vineyard so that we can work there (cf. Mt 20:1ff.). Jesus proposes to us the parables of the talents (Mt 25:14–30) or of the pounds (Lk 19:11–27). Deep-down, we are neither the originators nor the owners of anything, but merely the managers or stewards: we must see to it that the gifts received on active trust bear fruit. Even the most worldly possessions, even "dishonest money," must be used in such a way as to serve God and to assure ourselves the goods which no thief can take away (cf. Lk 16:1–13; Mt 6:19–21). Last of all, the activity which is demanded, if we are truly to find God, is pursued throughout the daily round of relations with other men. The words of the Lord about the last judgment, in Mt 25:31–46, do not belong in the genre of parable, yet their teaching is linked to the basic drive of the parables, as we shall see further on. They are, besides, confirmed by such parables as that of the good Samaritan (Lk 10:29ff.). The very theme of judgment is implied in many parables, like those of the steward, the ten maidens, the talents (Mt 24 and 25). The Lord will return. He will demand an accounting. He will render to each according to his works.[5]

In all these parables, God is made known less directly in Himself and for Himself than as the term of the rapport whose truth has been revealed to us so that we might achieve it. He who answered, when Moses asked His name: "I will be who I will be," you will know me by the things I will do for you (cf. Ex 3:14), is once again revealed by His action in our regard: He who saves the one who was lost. He is the one who summons sinners to return to Him and to share in His reign, He is the one who demands that He be preferred to all the rest, the one who respects our freedom to such an extent that we can make His advances come to nought, the one who is coming and whom

[5] Cf. Ps 62:13; Job 34:11; Mt 16:27 (cf. 13:39; 25:19f.); Lk 14:14; Rom 2:6, 12–16; 1 Cor 2:3, 8; 4:5; 2 Cor 5:10; 11:15; Eph 6:8; 1 Pet 1:17; Rev 2:23; 20:12; 22:12; cf. 14:15; 2 Tim 4:14.

114

we must be ready to receive, the one who asks men to freely and actively collaborate in achieving the result which will be crowned by Him alone, after He has called the effort forth, He is the one who will return, for He is Master of the whole temporal economy of the world. . . .

The Parables, Revelation of the "Heart" of Man

"Their ears are heavy of hearing"

From a literary standpoint, the parables are frequently wonderful little works. Having first tickled our curiosity, they charm us by their stories, by their features so finely observed and set forth. We get the inkling that there is something in them that we must figure out, some application of them that we must make. Each parable is a challenge: it is not simply a riddle, for it aims at getting the one who hears it into action; it puts him a question; better still, it puts *him* in question.

When the high priests and the pharisees are told the parable of the two sons sent by their father into the vineyard, or the one about the murderous vine-dressers, they are being asked to see themselves in the son with the willing words and the disobedient will, or in the vine-dressers who kill the servants and even the son of the master, so as to preserve their exploitation from interference.

Long since, under the former dispensation, the prophets had put forward similar parables. When David had had Uriah, Bathsheba's lawful husband, put to death, so that he could freely possess her, Nathan told him the tale of the rich man with many flocks and herds, who, to entertain a travelling friend, took the one little lamb, tenderly pampered, of a poor man. . . . "The man who has done this deserves to die!", David cried out. Nathan replied: "You are the man" (2 Sam 12:1ff.). A little later, a

115

woman of Tekoa, prompted by Joab, persuaded David to pardon his rebellious son Absalom by telling him the fictitious story of her son whom others sought to kill in revenge for his brother's death, of which he was guilty ... (2 Sam 14:1ff.).

The parables, then, are like a collection of mirrors in which I am invited to see myself in the underlying truth of my position. They lead me to put to myself this question: is it not I who received the seed of the Word as though on rocks, I who let it be choked by thorns? Is it not I who buried the talent, leaving it unproductive? Is it not I who am the priest or the levite who passed by, without bothering myself about the man who lay wounded alongside the road (Lk 10:29ff.)? Am I the rich man who was careless about his soul, or am I Lazarus, overwhelmed with disease (cf. Lk 16:19–31)? Do I pray with the same persistency as the importunate widow in Luke 18:1–8? When I ask myself questions like these, the parables reveal me to myself in those underlying inclinations which I, overly content with clinging to an easy tranquillity, had been deceiving myself about and had been careful to avoid bringing out into the open. They lead me to see myself as I am in respect of the religious rapport whose law or whose requirements they reveal. By means of them, I am, as it were, driven to make the decision and to give the answer I had been evading. I am personally summoned, brought back to the "heart," to that level of the conscience where man can no longer try to avoid the issue, no longer try to conceal his deepest needs by making a show of his possessions, where man is all but compelled to face himself, to see himself as he *is*, to give up the deceptive shelter of a spurious security, to take his stand in the direction of the ultimate realities. I am invited to that "immersing oneself deeper in existence" which Søren Kierkegaard saw as the necessary condition for entering truly into Christianity.[6]

6 *Concluding Unscientific Postscript*, Princeton, 1941, p. 497.

We see, then, that the parables combine two values: that of the revelation of the true religious rapport, and thus of the Kingdom of God, and that of the revelation of ourselves at the level of the "heart."[7] These two stages of revelation are ordered to one another and are made to meet. By means of the first, God comes to us; by means of the second, we are invited to make our way to Him. The parables, exactly like the "signs" (a category which is especially Johannine), are the places where a meeting is arranged, by means of a mutual advance of God and of human freedom. Truth comes towards us and offers itself; still veiled, it is nonetheless prepared, if we but begin to make ourselves open to it, to reveal more clearly what it is. When a man starts off with an inclination towards openness and from the very outset agrees to let himself be put in question, and then unreservedly seeks to hear the message addressed to him, however far his soul or the Truth itself might lead him, the Truth will disclose itself to him with ever greater fullness and he will grow in understanding: what is present is an openness of one to the other, an advance of one towards the other. "When a truth comes towards us and beckons even then, even though its incarnation in explicit idea has not yet been effected, a moment of decisive twilight occurs in which the future of the light depends upon the attitude, receptive or hostile, which we assume; the conclusion is there pre-formed incipiently: assent or refusal, self-surrender or rejection; and that is freedom's hour."[8] And the hour of grace as well.

On the precise point of the technique of the parables, our

[7] On the "heart" in the biblical sense of the word, which is, when all is said and done, its Pascalian sense, see *Encyclopedic Dictionary of the Bible*, New York, 1963, cols. 947–948; Claude TRESMONTANT, *A Study of Hebrew Thought*, New York, 1960; KITTEL, *TWNT*, vol. III, pp. 609–616.

[8] Edouard LE ROY, *Compte rendu de l'Académie des sciences morales et politiques*, 1936, p. 912. This psychology of the reciprocal advance of God and man was frequently and admirably expressed by St. GREGORY THE GREAT: *see Hom. 23 in Evang.*, I (*PL* 76, 1182); *In Ezech., lib.* I, hom. 7 (*PL* 76, 844f.).

Master, intent on achieving this reciprocal advance of God's truth and man's freedom, spoke these words: "To him who has will more be given, and he will have abundance; but from him who has not, even what he has will be taken away."[9] The Lord explained the full meaning of the parables to the disciples who followed Him and believed. But for the hearers "from without," still inattentive, hesitant, or even inaccessible, the obscurity and inadequacy which were characteristic of the parables had the effect of increasing the obscurity itself and brought about a still greater separation, while the potential light and the call to life which the parables offered withdrew and grew dim.[10] Both groups had at first been presented with the same *chiaroscuro* in which God offers to our freedom the opportunity of approach and revelation. Some, by their openness, had called forth the rising of a clearer light, while others, by their dullness, had provoked a still greater darkness or, more precisely, a still greater separation. There are some who have ears to hear and eyes to see, and others with ears not to hear, eyes not to see. The text from Isaiah 6:9–10, which we have met before, is thus fully confirmed: "They may indeed see but not perceive, and may indeed hear but not understand" (cf. Mk 4:12). The option is not offered only once; there are several stages in the reciprocal approach. The disciples, too, having begun to believe and thus to understand, could have paused along the way (cf. Mk 8:17–18). They were unceasingly invited to listen and to understand (cf. Mk 4:14 and 16): "Listen!" (4:3); "If any man has ears to hear, let him hear!" (4:23). We are constantly encountering what might be called the dialogical structure of the whole Bible

9 Mt 13:12; cf. Mk 4:25; Lk 8:18; 19:26; J. BUZY, *op. cit.,* p. 264.

10 The Fathers of the Church, the great scholastics, and their modern commentators rightly say that the first fault lies in not paying attention, in not exercising one's mind. Cf., e.g., St. AUGUSTINE, *De lib. arb.,* III, 22, 64 (PL 32, 1302); J. LAPORTE, "Le libre arbitre et l'attention selon saint Thomas," in *Revue de Métaphysique et de Morale,* 38 (1931), pp. 61–73; 39 (1932), pp. 199–223; 41 (1934), p. 25–57.

(the expression is one which is dear to Rabbi André Neher). The primary basis for it is in the creation of man "in the image" (Gen 1:26) and, in some way, as a *vis-à-vis* or partner of God. Man is, in very truth, capable of summons and response, of receiving or refusing a word from God. "We are indeed his offspring," says St. Paul (Acts 17:28).

The technique and method we have analyzed lead us to the recognition of a close relationship, tending towards a certain continuity, between their various stages. This can be confirmed no less from the standpoint of the content of the parables than from the standpoint of the stages which are crossed by the man who listens with good will, and which will lead to the faith of a disciple.

Leibniz said that the various orders of reality are mutually "symbolic": at the level of a lesser order, there are analogies of the higher. This is because the universe is one in origin, even though it was made in two phases (natural creation, covenant in grace). Monotheism in its fullness does not allow of the dualisms of separation at the level of created effects. Consequently, creation retains within itself a kind of "iconic" power and a possibility of turning into an "epiphany" of God. Still in all, pagan and sinful man fails to turn this power and possibility into the recognition of God and the praise of the Creator; this is why his eyes and his moral sense grow dim (on this subject, see St. Paul's words to the Romans, 1:18–32). But suppose God Himself comes to release and somehow to liberate the iconic or epiphanous power vested in things and in man himself? He came through His prophets and those whom He inspired, many times and in many ways: there is a Christian tradition which holds that the book of Scripture allows us to read the book of creation.[11] He came in His Son made man, the very One through whom, in His eternity, He made the world and all things (Heb 1:1–2). Jesus is, in the fullest sense of the word, the poet, who reveals the

[11] See the references in our *La Foi et la Théologie,* Paris, 1962, pp. 10–12.

119

poetic art of God: the sublime analogies which lie hidden in the simplest things. For Him, the world of things and of men is like a lyre which He plays and by whose strains He leads us to the threshold of the things of God. Everything can be a parable. All that is required to bring forth its captive truth is a prophet, a poet, *vates*. Parables, in the mind of Jesus and on His lips, are not just a teaching technique, nor even just the prudent progress by which the Truth offers itself to the free acceptance of men. The parables are as well, and profoundly, the translation of His experience, of His *true* reading of the world.[12]

When a man is offered an approach to God by way of things, images, parables, or "signs," he undergoes a transition, through a kind of psychologically increasing ascent, from the natural to grace. This follows from the fact that the future attitudes of the disciple, or of the indifferent man, or, at the worst, of the rebel, are foreshadowed from the very start in the basic dispositions which determine the initial reception or exclusion. It remains always possible, of course, for a change, a breaking-off, a spiritual newness to occur. Whether it is parables or "signs" that are at issue, "the relationship which man has acquired with the truth prior to his contact with Jesus determines his ability to believe in Jesus."[13] In the accession to full supernatural faith, there is a faith prior to faith, one which basically consists in an attitude both moral and psychological; there are (actual) graces prior to Grace, an openness and obedience which foreshadow those of the disciple. The way is travelled according to the same laws which

---

[12] Compare K. DELHAYE, *Erneuerung der Seelsorgsformen aus der Sicht der Frühen Patristik,* Freiburg, 1958, pp. 13–14. —Compare Paul CLAUDEL, *Art poétique,* Paris, 1915; Michel CARROUGES, "La nature est une parole," in *La Maison-Dieu,* no. 22 (1950/2), pp. 19–43. In a study of the parables of the Kingdom or of the evangelical "signs," it would be proper to show in more precise fashion how the natural realities evoked possess an objective similarity to the things of the Kingdom of grace—somewhat like Maurice Blondel's emphasis, in the religious miracle, on the presence of something extraordinary in the natural order, which signifies the extraordinary of the philanthropy and *agapē of God.*

[13] Friedrich BUCHSEL, *Die Johannesbriefe,* Leipzig, 1933, pp. 20–21.

govern at the very end, and leads there only if the end is already present and somehow anticipated in the antecedent stages. Jesus is already the way which leads to Himself, grasped in all His fullness. It is this type of anticipation of the term in its preparations and approaches which provides the ontological basis of the truth of Newman's psychological analysis in his theory of the "illative sense" or sense of inferences.

A correspondence exists between the stages of approach through the "heart" and the stages of disclosure of the meaning of the parable. As the object is being revealed, man is getting to the root of himself. A truly reciprocal conditioning takes place within the mutual advances of which we have spoken.

All of this finds verification especially on the level of personal destiny. Free acts point up individual persons. The Lord appeals to John or to Paul, but it is they who determine their response according to the dispositions of their hearts and the insistency of the Lord in bringing them to commit themselves. The history of the Truth and the history of souls are not matters which are closed off. The parables of the Gospels, uttered just once and brought down to us through the testimony of the apostles, still encounter and arouse today the same reactions of indifference, of inattention, or of desire and of surrender. They still bring about conversions. Some are the conversions of the faithful who listen, year after year, to the parables being read and meditate on them; such conversions are innumerable, but they are modest, discreet, gradual rather than sudden. Other conversions are sudden in the extreme. Father Th. Mainage tells the story of one such conversion, recounted to him by Adolphe Retté. Retté had known a young physician who had been quite bowled over, really turned inside out, by reading, during an idle stroll along the quais of Paris, the parable of the prodigal son and the chapter on the Good Shepherd.[14]

But the Gospel was, and always has been, a *public* preaching. The parables were proposed to the crowds. The Lord was hitting

14 Th. MAINAGE, *La Psychologie de la conversion*, Paris, 1915, pp. 333f.

out against a kind of collective lack of intelligence. If we make exception for the variations in personal freedoms, we can transpose to historical periods or collectivities the analysis of the attitudes of openness or of exclusion which we have outlined. Newman, reviewing the general situation in the nineteenth century, keenly applied to it the analyses Pascal had made—on the level of the individual conscience—of the way a man declares himself either in the direction of faith or in a contrary direction, and thereby induces the victory or failure of the light, mixed with obscurities, which faith presents.[15]

From all this, it follows that a preaching in parables is, in some way or other, a permanent function of the Christian Word. What Jesus did long ago, at a precise point in time and space, must be effected for men of all ages by the Christian apostolate. All men must be brought into the presence of the generating cause of faith—with the interior summons and the help of grace —which is what the parable-word is. They must be brought into the presence of an approach of the Truth which offers itself to the decision of their "heart" and which begins, if they will it, the advance of one towards the other: by means of a clearer declaration on the part of the Word, and a more definite openness and deepening awareness on the part of men. How ardently might a preacher wish to be a minister of the Gospel in this wise, fully conscious that "a disciple is not above his teacher, nor is the one who is sent above the one who has sent him" (Mt 10:24; Lk 6:40). The sower of the Gospel word breathes forth a fervent prayer in rereading, this time without any literary orientation, the words of Paul Claudel which are so powerfully evocative of the mystery of the proclamation of the Kingdom in parables:

Let me be among men like a fellow without a face and my
    Word in them quite soundless like a sower of silence, soundless, a
sower of shadows, soundless, a sower of churches,

[15] See J.-H. WALGRAVE, *Newman the Theologian*, New York, 1960, pp. 148f.

122

Like a sower of the measure of God.
Like a tiny seed with an unknown name
Which, cast in good earth, takes in all its strength and brings forth
a plant that is special,
Complete with all its roots and all,
Just so the word in the soul. Speak then, O lifeless earth which lies
between my fingers!
Let me be like a sower of solitude and let him who hears my word
Return to his home restless and slow. . . .[16]

Is our preaching enough like that? Does the Church make
enough of the power of the parables to effect the approach of
God? Does our theology of the Word of God, so little more than
embryonic, make us sufficiently aware that the Word brings
into intimate contact living Truth and free consciences? By the
very fact that it is proposed, the Word is both the occasion and
the means through which a kind of judgment of the world is
made, for it sets forth a fact in whose regard men assume some
attitude, an attitude which judges them. If I set forth the fact
of Jesus Christ, if I make present an approach of the Kingdom,
those who listen to me are no longer innocent: they assume some
position, either in the direction of the justice which follows upon
faith, or in the direction of culpable rejection, though it be but
from inattentiveness. Once again, the text from Isaiah takes on
an awesome actuality. By preaching, I celebrate the mystery of
salvation which, once missed, becomes perdition. Am I really
aware of what is at stake? Am I, for my own part, sufficiently
committed to the Gospel? Have I lived seriously enough the
blessed and dramatic tension of the dialogue by which one becomes a disciple? Have I sufficiently nourished my life with
the Word, and the Word with my life? And if, after listening to
the voice of the Lord, I listen to the voice of those who have
witnessed to Him, do I not realize how far indeed I am, when all
is said and done, from what Ignatius Martyr tells me it is to be a
true disciple: not some *sound* or other, *phonē,* however pleasing

[16] *Cinq Grandes Odes,* La Maison fermée, Paris, 1936, p. 148.

to the ear, but in very truth a *voice*, a *word*, *logos*, through a total existential commitment to the following of Christ.[17]

The Parables in the Economy of Salvation

The parables are a semi-obscure and semi-clear way to propose the truth. They demand some effort of understanding and explanation. We have seen the dialogical structure, the exchange, the reciprocity, here involved. It is a structure which implies delays, both those which are common to any exchange and those which are required for the declaration of our intentions and the exercise of our freedom. All the way through, the parables, exactly like the "signs," fit very well into an economy in which our freedom must unfold and declare itself. This is something which can be understood by means of the analogy of love.

Today, Ellen put a bright yellow headband on her chestnut hair. She knows that she is going to meet Roger. She says to herself: if he feels about me as I feel about him, he will understand. Possibly he will not even notice: Ellen will leave it at that. If Roger perceives its charm—the sign of a still more intimate advance—a love which is just beginning will discover other ways of asserting itself and of calling forth a response. A simple sign, a signal: if he loves me, he will understand! The sign is the means which is best-adapted to lead someone to declare himself, should he be so inclined, while completely respecting the spontaneous character of his freedom. The first step inaugurates the play of reciprocal and progressive advances of which we have spoken. It has some content already, and is already in the pattern of what it will lead to, if recognized and received. The most subtle leads of love prefigure love itself.

[17] St. IGNATIUS OF ANTIOCH, *Rom.* II, 1, in the edition of A. Lelong, Paris, 1910. Père CAMELOT, in *Sources chrétiennes*, 10, Paris, 1944, follows a simpler text, which avoids the "subtle distinctions" of the text admitted by preceding editors. But the distinction between *logos* and *phōnē* is well known in Christian literature, particularly at Alexandria: cf. M. HARL, *Origène et la fonction révélatrice du Verbe incarné*, Paris, 1958, pp. 78, 312.

This convention of a summons made to a freedom one does not wish to hurry in any way absolutely demands the light-and-shade of sign or parable. Enough light is needed so that some meaning can be perceived, but there is also need for enough semi-obscurity or ambiguity to rule out any constraint and to insure that the response is freely formed according to the dispositions of our "heart." God too presents His message in such a way that there can be some justification for not understanding it and for rejecting it, while a real possibility of recognizing and accepting it remains. This was the view of Pascal and, after him, of Kierkegaard. Pascal expressed what he so deeply felt in language one cannot hope to better:

> It was not right that Jesus Christ should appear in a manner which was divine and absolutely capable of convincing all men; but neither was it right that He should come in a manner so hidden that He could not be known by those who sought Him sincerely. He wanted to make Himself perfectly recognizable to these. And so, willing to appear plainly to those who sought Him with all their heart, He shades His knowledge, so as to give visible signs of Himself to those who sought Him and not to those who sought Him not. There is light enough for those whose only desire is to see, and obscurity enough for those whose disposition is otherwise.[18]

There are signs and parables whose source is positive revelation, but, for those who are chosen, all is grace; everything can

[18] *Pensées,* No. 430. Compare nos. 557, 588, etc. PASCAL himself applies this rule of faith to the coming of Jesus Christ (nos. 567, 588), to the senses of Scripture (no. 571), to the proclamation it makes of Jesus Christ (no. 578).

In *Training in Christianity* (1850), KIERKEGAARD comments on the saying of our Lord, "When I am lifted up from the earth, I will draw all to myself," and gives to it an interpretation which is the same as that given by DOSTOEVSKI in the "Legend of the Grand Inquisitor." Kierkegaard says that a man is primarily and authentically himself in his free choice. If, in one way or another, Jesus were to force men, He would not draw (*drage*) them but would deceive (*bedrage*) them; it would not be *they* whom He was gaining, but a kind of impersonal machine. (There is an English translation of *Training in Christianity* by Walter Lowrie, Princeton, 1944; see pp. 159–161.)

be sign and parable for those whom God calls and who do not refuse to seek Him. The crucial choices in our lives take shape in the whole framework of life; salvation is played out in a position which we adopt in respect of everything, even when we do not really know that the final stakes are so high. Basically, God is a hidden God, or, better, He turns up in all the realities of existence which call forth from us a declaration of our fundamental dispositions. Many passages from the Bible are eloquent on this score. Abraham saw three travellers coming towards him; in giving them hospitality, he did not know that he was receiving "angels," indeed God Himself. . . . When a man named Simon, who came from Cyrene, was returning from the fields on the afternoon before the feast of the Passover, and was made by the Roman soldiers to carry the cross of a condemned man who could not drag it along himself, he had no idea that he was carrying the instrument of the world's salvation, on his Lord's account. According to the teaching of Mt 25:31–46, when men appear for the judgment, they are amazed to learn that, in giving food to the needy, they had nourished God Himself, and that, in refusing clothing to those in want, they had left naked and exposed to the biting cold their Lord and Saviour. In the last analysis, we never know what it is we do. The visits of God are mingled darkness and light. Often, our freedom is orientated without our being fully conscious of where it will issue. The essential thing is the orientation we take. Even though it be taken solely in respect of men, on a level which seems purely natural, if the orientation is one of openness and of love, it already foreshadows and implies an attitude taken in regard to Christ and to God, who is Love.[19]

Indeed, we never really know what it is we do, and it is

[19] See our *The Wide World My Parish. Salvation and Its Problems,* Baltimore, 1961, pp. 117f.; compare W. GROSSOUW, *Pour mieux comprendre saint Jean,* Paris-Bruges, 1946, pp. 33f.

because of this, because the choice has not been made with an absolutely unexceptionable light, that sins committed against the Son of man can be pardoned.[20] God's ways are always truth and justice and mercy.

[20] This is how A. FEUILLET interprets Mt 12:31–32 and Lk 12:10 ("Le discours de Jésus sur la ruine du Temple," in *RB*, 56, 1949, p. 65, n. 2).

Third Part

Christ the Lord

1

Christ, Invisible Leader
of the Visible Church

According to St. Paul

1. *Christ-as-Leader*. St. Paul's idea of Christ-as-Leader. Content of the notion of "*kephalē*." Domain over which Christ is Head. Relationship of Christ as Leader to His body which is the Church.

2. *Christ, Invisible Leader of the Visible Church*. A) *He is* truly *the Leader*. 1. The fact. Reality of His action. 2. Christ-as-Leader in the gift of grace. The Sacred Heart. 3. The Church is built from and in heaven. B) *Christ is* the invisible *Leader of the visible Church*. Dogmatic knowledge. Catholic teaching and Protestant theology. The members of the Church.

1. Christ-as-Leader

During the last thirty years or so, exegetes have frequently dealt with the theme of Christ-*kephalē* as it is related to that of the *Sôma* (*Christoú*).[1] Although complete agreement among the

---

[1] In point of fact, the notion of *sôma* has been far more extensively studied, while *kephalē* has been studied only *in obliquo*. Besides the commentaries on Colossians (M. MEINERTZ, Bonn, 1931) and Ephesians (H. SCHLIER, Düsseldorf, 1958), we should cite the following studies (the

authors does not exist, a trend towards consensus on a number
of important points is noticeable. It is necessary that theologians
be kept *au courant* of exegetical research and results. Where they
are not, there is a danger of creating in the realm of the sacred
sciences a quite unhealthy situation of "double truth," with each
science pursuing its own dialogue in ignorance of the rest. Now
it is by no means rare that eminent theologians will start with
a notion of "head"—traditional, perhaps, or at least traditional in
part—without having examined it in the light of modern
exegesis, a science whose resources are, after all, superior to
those at the disposal of the Fathers and the scholastics. In point
of fact, where the findings of philology have been investigated
and respected, philology has from time to time brought new
vigor to certain chapters in theology. Starting, in scholastic
fashion, with the notions of head and body, a number of treatises
illustrate the various aspects of these notions with biblical cita-

asterisk indicates those in which we have found special support for our
argument): H. SCHLIER, "Die Kirche nach dem Epheserbrief," in *Catholica*,
1949; *Id.*, article "Kephalē," in *TWNT*, vol. III, pp. 672–681*; A.
WIKENHAUSER, *Die Kirche als mystische Leib nach d. Apostel Paulus*,
Münster, 1937; J. DEIMEL, *Leib Christi. Sinn und Grenzen einer Deutung
des innerkirchlichen Lebens*, Freiburg, 1940 (pp. 128f., critique of the
Käsemann-Schlier interpretation); E. PERCY, *Der Leib Christi (Sōma
Christou) in den paulinischen Homologumena u. Antilogomena*, Lund-
Leipzig, 1942; L. CERFAUX, *The Church in the Theology of St. Paul*, New
York, 1959; L. MALEVEZ, "L'Eglise, Corps du Christ. Sens et provenance
de l'expression chez saint Paul," in *Sciences Religieuses* (= *RechScRel*, 32),
1944, pp. 27–94*; J. DUPONT, *Gnosis. La connaissance religieuse dans les
épîtres de saint Paul*, Louvain, 1949, pp. 445f.*; W. GOOSSENS, *L'Eglise,
Corps du Christ d'après saint Paul*, Paris, 1949; Th. SOIRON, *Die Kirche
als der Leib Christi nach d. Lehre d. hl. Paulus* . . . , Düsseldorf, 1951; P.
MICHALON, "L'Eglise, Corps mystique du Christ glorieux," in *NRT*, 74
(1952), pp. 673–687; J. A. T. ROBINSON, *The Body. A Study in Pauline
Theology* (Studies in Biblical Theology, 5), London, 1952; J. M. GONZALEZ
RUIZ, "Sentido soteriologico de Kephalē en la Cristologia de San Pablo," in
Anthologia Annua, I, Rome, 1953, pp. 185–224; P. BENOIT, "*Corps, Tête
et Plérôme dans les* Epîtres de la Captivité," in *RB*, 63 (1956), pp. 5–44
(reprinted in *Exégèse et Théologie*, Paris, 1961, vol. II, pp. 107–153
(references in this volume. We owe a great deal to Benoit's study.)*; P.
BONNARD, "L'Eglise-corps du Christ dans le paulinisme," in *Revue de
Théologie et de Philosophie*, 1958, pp. 268–282.

132

tions whose exact textual meaning may very well be neither in point nor in the precise Pauline perspective. Analogous remarks could be made on several other notions, some of which are extremely important.

St. Paul's idea of Christ-as-Leader

The first question we should ask is how the notion of Christ-as-Leader comes up in St. Paul. Pierre Benoit seems to have proposed some illuminating remarks on the subject. Prior to the captivity epistles (putting to one side 1 Cor 12:21, where the head is mentioned, along with other members, in the context of an application to the Christian community of the classic sociological theme of the body), the notion appears just once, in 1 Cor 11:3, without any intrinsic relationship to the theme of the body of Christ (a theme which is, however, already present in the great epistles): "The head of every man is Christ, the head of a woman is her husband, and the head of Christ is God." *Kephalē* has here the meaning of "authority over" and connotes the first principle or origin, by reason of the text's allusion to the account of the creation (Eve drawn forth from Adam).[2] It is clear that *kephalē* will readily lend itself to composition with the notion of body in the context of the theology of Christ as principle of the Christian life. It is also clear that its primary value in the thought of St. Paul is not as the principal member of the bodily organism, but as authority.[3]

As early as First Corinthians and Romans, St. Paul puts forward his idea of the bodily union of Christians in the paschal

[2] Cf. verses 7 and following; SCHLIER, *TWNT*, III, p. 678.
[3] St. JOHN CHRYSOSTOM, the most exegetically minded of the Fathers, strongly insists on this value and readily speaks in terms of *archē*. Cf. *In Ephes.*, c. 1, hom. 1, 4; hom. 3, 2–3; c. 4, hom. 10, 1 (*PG* 62, 16, 26f., 75f.); *In 2 Thess.*, c. 3, hom. 5, 5 (*PG* 62, 499f.).

body of Christ.[4] He makes no departure from the well-known illustration of the members, but utilizes it simply to invite Christians to preserve the union *among themselves,* a union which they must preserve because radically they are, on the foundation of baptism and the Eucharist, one with the sacrificed and risen Christ. And yet, neither in First Corinthians nor in Romans does St. Paul express the relationship maintained by Christ with His ecclesial body in terms of *kephalē:* 1 Cor 12:21 indicates that this category holds no place in his thinking at the time.

The idea of Christ-as-Leader comes up in the captivity epistles, Colossians and Ephesians (dating from 61–63), in a fashion thematically independent of the notion of body-*sôma,* and not as an elaboration of the notion analytically inferred from the internal nature of the body, which as such properly calls for a head. The idea comes up, thematically, in the context of the critique of a certain gnosis, or pre-gnosis, which had infected Christian circles in that corner of "Asia" or Phrygia. What was involved was not the beginning of a philosophical gnosis, properly speaking (despite Col 2:8), but the spread of ideas which had developed in certain Jewish religious currents, of which the Qumran texts offer a parallel, and perhaps even a source. Involved were the reintroduction of Jewish observances (circumcision, dietary practices: Col 2:11–13, 16, 21), the celebration of certain feasts and days (Col 2:16), along with worship of the angels and, undoubtedly, speculation on their role in the religious economy (Col 2:8; Eph 2:2; cf. Eph 6:12).

To counteract the seductiveness of such theses, St. Paul maintains that Christ is above the powers, first in respect of the

[4] Cf. 1 Cor 6:11–20; 10:17; 12:12–27; Rom 12:4–5; BENOIT, *op. cit.,* p. 116. On the body as paschal, C. F. D. MOULE, "Sanctuary and Sacrifice in the Church of the New Testament," in *JTS,* 1950, pp. 29–41. On the allegory of the members, A. WIKENHAUSER, *op. cit.,* pp. 130–143; W. NESTLE, "Die Fabel des Menenius Agrippa," in *Klio,* 21 (1926–1927), pp. 358f.; *Griechische Studien,* 1948, pp. 502f.

thrones, dominions, principalities, powers (Col 1:15f.), their
vanquisher (2:15; Phil 2:9f.). "God has made him the head
over all things for the church."[5] As a result, we who are consecrated to Christ are religiously emancipated from everything
which has been subjected to Him and which some have again
desired to make principles of the religious rapport.

Content of the notion of "kephalē"

The primary meaning implied by the notion of *kephalē* is not
that of internal principle of an organism—either in the realm
of its life (physiology) or in the realm of its structure (morphology)—but that of being above, of holding the summit.
To be the leader above is to have all things under one's feet,
Eph 1:22 (Ps 8:6). As we have seen, this is the sense in which
the affirmation of Christ-as-Leader is first presented, cf. 1 Cor
11:3: the husband is the leader of his wife, who depends on
him and, in the acknowledgment of this dependence, is like
his reflection, his image, his representation, his *doxa*. It is in
this way that the Church is subject to Christ, who is her leader,
Eph 5:23–24.

Placed at the summit, the *kephalē* is first: Col 1:15–18.
This primacy is not chronological only, but ontological as well:
the First is also Principle, so that He who is *Kephalē toû sōmatos,
tês ekklesías,* is also *archē* and *en pâsin Proteúon* (Col 1:18–19).
In the New Testament, there is always a correspondence between
the mysterious *in se* of God and the salvific activity exerted by
God, between theology and the economy. Christ, in particular,
is never considered or affirmed without a role in relationship to
men or to the world. This is the basic conviction of St. Paul and
it dominates everything he says about the Body of Christ: what

[5] Eph 1:21–22. The Vulgate's translation, "*super omnem Ecclesiam,*" is
bad: cf. T. ZAPELENA, *De Ecclesia Christi.* Pars altera, apologetico-dogmatica,
Rome, 2nd ed., 1954, pp. 385, 428.

Christ is, what He experienced and did, concerns all men and even the whole cosmos, *Ta Panta*. Thus, by nature First over all, Christ-as-Leader is also Principle. Other texts from the New Testament show Him to us as Principle, *archē*, of creation (Rev 3:14), of revelation (Jn 8:25; cf. Heb 1:1–4), of resurrection (1 Cor 15:20). Principle, He is nonetheless End, the End through whom and for whom all things exist (1 Cor 8:6; Rom 11:36; Heb 2:10). He thus constitutes something like a space within being, a reference both of origin and of finality, in relation to which it is possible to receive a new existence (*"in Christo"* . . .).

We know that the expression *"anakephalaïosis,"* "recapitulation," in Eph 1:10, is not derived from *"kephalē,"* "head," but from *"kephalaïon,"* which denotes the summit, the principal part of a thing in which all the rest is summed up. The corresponding verb denotes: to sum up, to contract something into its essential elements. The immediate meaning, then, is not to "re-head," to reassume under a new leader. And yet, there are eminent exegetes who do not hesitate to take this as the *real* meaning of the expression, beyond its strict philological derivation.[6] The fact is that the two meanings converge. The meaning of the Pauline expression, well perceived by the Fathers,[7] is this: to sum up all things by instituting the summit, *kephalaïon*, without permitting anything to be lost from any one (*ana*). Christ is the summit, the farthest limit of creation, where everything converges as in its final realization. But if the primary meaning of *kephalē* is that of First, summit, and not that of vital princi-

---

[6] This is the position taken by SCHLIER, *TWNT*, III, p. 682; CERFAUX, *The Church in the Theology of St. Paul*, p. 314, n. 30; J. DUPONT, *op. cit.*, p. 425; BENOIT, *op. cit.*, p. 138, n. 2; etc.

[7] Cf. J. M. DUFORT, "La récapitulation paulinienne dans l'exégèse des Pères," in *Sciences ecclésiastiques*, 12 (1960), pp. 21–38; compare P. VAN IMSCHOOT, "Recapitulare omnia in Christo," in *Collat. Gandav.*, 29 (1946), p. 5.

ple, still we can concede that over and above *kephalaïon,* and even by reason of it, St. Paul linked up the theme of *anakephalaïosis* to the capacity as *kephalē* which belonged to Christ. First over all, Principle of all, Christ was like the limit of all creation, newly receiving and realizing its meaning according to God, which is the positive reality of salvation. The plan of God was to give to the world a principle of salvation by instituting at its summit an incorruptible compendium of all creation, in which creation would have the principle of a new departure: in somewhat the same way as humanity had been saved in a compendium of itself, in the family of Noah.

To express, or even to explain, this function of universal principle of salvation, St. Paul made use of the expression "*plērōma.*" It is difficult to find an image for this notion. For St. Paul himself, it is unquestionably a formula which corresponds to an extremely rich image which he failed to express either clearly or fully, but in which he combined both an Old Testament theology of wisdom, of *Shekinah* or Presence, and stoic ideas which had been widely popularized in his day. Although we are here unable to justify, by detailed analysis, an interpretation which has taken form as a result of improved and more recent studies,[8] we can say this by way of *résumé:* the Pauline notion of *plērōma* would best be translated by combining the idea of totality with the overtones, both quantitative and qualitative, of the word "dimension" in contemporary English usage: we speak, for example, of "a certain dimension" of being or of thought. . . . What is involved is the restoration to things of a certain being according to God. This is the object of the plan of God ("the mystery of his will," "benevolent purpose," Eph 1:9; "pre-

---

[8] Besides the studies of E. PERCY, J. DUPONT, H. SCHLIER (*Die Kirche nach dem Epheserbrief*), P. BENOIT, cited in note 1, cf. Fr. MUSSNER, *Christus, das All und die Kirche. Studien zur Theologie des Epheserbriefes,* Trier, 1955; A. FEUILLET, "L'Eglise plérôme du Christ d'après Ephes. I, 23," in *NRT,* 78 (1956), pp. 449–472, 593–610.

ordained plan," Eph 1:11; "mystery," Eph 3:3, 4, 9); a plan which was formed by "the manifold wisdom unfolded by God according to this eternal purpose," Eph 3:10–11. The plan of divine wisdom is to restore to the world a being-according-to-God, through Christ, by making the whole dwell in Christ as in its summit, principle, and summing-up, as in its summit-summary. The position of Christ, thus become filled by the whole, Paul calls *plērōma* (Col 1:19; 2:9). It is thus that men, and then, with men, all things, can be associated with the fullness which, first found in Christ, the head of all things, is communicated from Him to us and to all (Col 2:10). Christ becomes, for Christians and for the world, the principle of participation in the whole. This is a participation in a new being-according-to-God, a filial being, and in a restored ontology, a saved whole. When one is filled from God through Christ, he is integrated into the whole which is the saved world (Eph 3:19; Col 2:10). For men, this is achieved, on the foundation of baptism, by the faith and love which make up the Church. So it is that the Church, after Christ and from Him, becomes the *plērōma;* she becomes, after Christ Himself, the body of the whole, that is, of an existence according to God which is possible for all things.[9] She is this for all things, *Ta panta,* which, from God through Christ and from Christ through the Church, can become once more the whole in which the presence of God dwells. Thus they can reëxist according to God, as sons.

Christ's place in the plan of divine wisdom is elsewhere expressed in other terms or categories which signify in another fashion *realities* which are closely connected, if not identical in all respects. Here, as before, Christ appears as the one whom the Father has consecrated and sent into the world (Jn 10:36) to

---

[9] "*He has put all things under his feet* and has made him the head over all things for the church, which is his body, the fulness of him who fills all in all" (Eph 1:22–23); "For in him the whole fulness of deity dwells bodily, and you have come to fulness of life in him . . ." (Col. 2:9–10).

CHRIST, INVISIBLE LEADER OF THE VISIBLE CHURCH

"save the world," that is, to give to the world the possibility of renewing its being according to God. Christ is the means by whom God exercises His sovereignty of grace, and thus truly acts as God, in relation to His creatures, by bringing to its conclusion, in spite of sin, the purpose He had designed for them: cf. Jn 3:16–17, 35; 17:2. From this follow the texts in the First Letter to the Corinthians, where the category of "New (Last) Adam" is the equivalent of *Kephalē-Archē*:[10] "For us there is only one God, the Father, from whom are all things and for whom we exist, and only one Lord, Jesus Christ, through whom all things exist and through whom we are [or: through whom we are going]";[11] "In Christ shall all be made alive. But each in his own order: Christ the first fruits, then those who belong to Christ. . . . Then comes the end, when he delivers the kingdom to God the Father after destroying every rule and every authority and power. . . . When all things are subjected to him, then the Son himself will also be subjected to him who put all things under him, that God may be everything to every one" (1 Cor 15:23–28).[12]

Domain over which Christ is Head

Again and again, in his letters to the Colossians and the Ephesians, St. Paul combines two assertions concerning the domain over which Christ is Leader: on the one hand, everything, *Ta Panta* (Col 1:15–18), *ê kephalē páses archês kaì exousías*

---

[10] Christ is the image of the substance of the Father, the heir of all things and the one through whom "God" made the world: Col 1:15; 2 Cor 4:4; Heb 1:2–3. He makes Him known: Jn 1:18; 14:6–10ᵃ.

[11] 1 Cor 8:6 (compare Col 1:16). M. M. SAGNARD, in a note in *Ephem. Theol. Lovan.*, 26 (1950), pp. 54–58, suggests the following translation: "Yet for us (there is but) one sole God, the Father, from whom <come> all things and towards whom we <are going>—and one sole Lord Jesus Christ through whom <come> all things and through whom we are going."

[12] Jesus Christ *panta kai en pasin* (Col 3:11) is the means for the realization of God (the Father) as *panta en pasin* (1 Cor 15:28).

(2:10), *Kephalèn hupèr Pánta* (Eph 1:22); on the other, the Church, *ē Kephalē toû Sōmatos, tês ekklesías* (Col 1:18; compare 2:19); "He has made him the leader [over all things] for the Church" (Eph 1:22). Or, again, Christ is the first-born of all creation (Col 1:15), but, on the other hand, the first-born from the dead (Col 1:18; 1 Cor 15:20).

There exist, then, something like two concentric zones in the domain over which Christ is leader. One is of absolutely universal extent, embracing everything created, even the cosmic or angelic powers which are ultimately hostile to the reign of God (Col 2:10; Eph 1:21f.; etc.); the other, made up of men who accept the Gospel and which is properly speaking the Church, is presented by St. Paul, starting with the period of the great epistles, as the body of Christ. The cosmos, the "everything" is not called the body of Christ, but it comes under Christ-as-Leader inasmuch as He thus comprehends and contains *everything* (*plērōma*), and is capable of bestowing its meaning on everything and of subjecting to Himself, even that which resists Him. The Church, on the other hand, is the body of Christ, the unified assembly of men who, having by faith accepted Christ as their master, have been united to His paschal body, His body of death and resurrection, offered and glorified, through baptism and the Eucharist. Christ is its *kephalē* in a new and original sense, something which goes beyond the prior sense. How so? This is what we are going to attempt to clarify.

Relationship of Christ-as-Leader to His body which is the Church

St. Paul did not introduce the theme of Christ-as-Leader by means of an elaboration of the idea of Church-as-Body (of Christ). But from the moment the two themes were combined and placed in relationship to one another, they could not remain simply juxtaposed. Not only was Christ the Leader of the

140

Church in a fashion other than that in which He was Leader of the cosmic whole, but, since the Church was Christ's Body, His status as *kephalē* had necessarily to assume a distinct value by reason of its being combined with *sôma,* body.

The relationship which exists between the two is not the relationship found between head and trunk which together form a complete man. The schema *Christus totus, Christus integer, unus homo,* which was inherited from Tyconius by St. Augustine, and from St. Augustine by the medieval West, has the disadvantage of leading towards that conclusion. Its real substance, however, and one which is extremely rich, manages to overcome this disadvantage very well. Furthermore, principally for reasons of method, what St. Augustine[13] included within the notion of *caput* as applied to Christ with regard to His body was not the value of communication of grace—something which was reserved, in his mind, to God or to Christ as God (*"in forma Dei," "secundum Majestatem"*)—but the following values: 1. In Christ is the fullness of wisdom and of grace, just as there is in the head the fullness of the senses, while the rest of the body has only the sense of touch; 2. Christ is the model and *Rector,* the supreme governor of His Church; 3. He is the *cause,* in His humanity, only of bodily effects.

The body of Christ which is the Church is not related to its leader as the trunk is to the head. The Semitic notion of "body," which was certainly St. Paul's notion, included the idea of place or sphere, as well as the idea of a means of making manifest

---

[13] See on this subject G. PHILIPS, "L'influence du Christ-Chef sur son Corps mystique suivant saint Augustin," in *Augustinus Magister,* Paris, 1954, pp. 805f.; S. TROMP, *Corpus Christi quod est Ecclesia,* II, *De Christo Capite Mystici Corporis,* Rome, 1960, pp. 39f.; 231–234. We have also studied the question, following particularly the exegesis of Jn 1:16, "*de plenitudine omnes nos accepimus,*" and have arrived at conclusions which are in agreement with those of the authors cited. The Church is ruled by Christ as is a body by its head: St. AUGUSTINE, *De nuptiis et concupiscentia,* I, 20, 22 (*PL* 44, 427).

the action of a personal principle.[14] The body of Christ is the communicating assembly of men in whom, through faith, baptism, and the Eucharist, Christ really effects what He Himself experienced, once for all, in His body in behalf of all: His paschal mystery. The Church is the sphere in which Christ corporeally communicates to the believer his own paschal destiny of death and resurrection. It is thus that the Church is the body of Christ, the effective realization and manifestation of the living personal principle, now hidden in God, who is the (dead and) glorified Christ. We do well to recall here St. Paul's first use of *kephalē*, in 1 Cor 11:3f.: if man is the head of woman, she is the glory of man, reflecting and manifesting his image.[15]

Christ, as *kephalē* of the Church, is first of all the Leader who possesses authority over her. The powers of vital influx and interiority should not make us forget this aspect, which is primary and perdures. Christ is First, the Principle, *Archē* (Col 1:18), and in a thoroughgoing way, in respect of everything which makes up the Church His body, its external structure no less than its intimate life. For the latter as for the former, Christ contains within Himself, as the peak of a cone contains its entire development, the fullness of all that will be unfolded in the body.

The authority which Christ exercises over His body-Church has a completely different character from the authority He exercises over the cosmos, so as to subject it to Himself, and, with all the more reason, over the rebellious powers, so as to constrain them. This authority is one which is, in fact, exercised

[14] To the studies mentioned above, note 1, should be added (cf. WIKENHAUSER, p. 103: MALEVEZ, pp. 83f.; ROBINSON, p. 14: BENOIT, p. 111): J. BONSIRVEN, *L'Evangile de Paul,* Paris, 1948, pp. 222–223, and particularly the excellent article by W. HILLMANN, "Die Kirche in der neutestl. Glaubensverkündigung," in *Liturgie und Mönchtum,* 3, Folge, H. 17, Maria Laach, 1955, pp. 18–33.

[15] Compare, in 1 Cor 15:40f., the relationship between *sôma* and *doxa.*

within an order of personal relationships, and its effect is *received* in a loving obedience. It is this which makes of it, as to Christ, an authority of tenderness and of generosity, one which extends even to the sacrifice of Himself (Eph 5:21–33). As for the Church, by receiving the action and by following the desires of her Lord, she is conformed and assimilated to Him, and truly becomes His image—something which can hardly be said of the cosmos, and still less of the rebellious forces, which will do no more than submit to the authority of their Lord (cf. the formula in exorcism: "*Recognosce sententiam tuam*" ...).

Christ-*kephalē* is both principle and end of the life and growth of His body: "We are to grow up in every way *into* him who is the Head, into Christ, *from whom* the whole body, joined and knit together by every joint with which it is supplied, when each part is working properly, makes bodily growth and upbuilds itself in love."[16] The heavenly and glorified Christ is present in His Church, and produces within her the holiness which He hopes to find there at His glorious return: 1 Thess 3:12–13; compare Eph 4:16, texts which deserve to be reread in this connection. The entire body receives from Christ, its *kephalē*—elsewhere called by St. Paul *ho Kyrios*, Eph 6:9—an influx of life, thanks to which it grows in love, in such a way as to tend effectively towards rejoining the Head, towards equalling it:[17] the body grows towards the Head.

Christ-*kephalē* is, for His body, the standard of existence and of life. Growth takes place according to the structures which He has arranged: St. Paul calls them *aphai*, joints (Eph 4:16), and also *sundesma*, ligaments (Col 2:19), expressions which are borrowed from the medical science of Hippocrates and

[16] Eph 4:15–16, compare 2:15f., 21–22 and 4:12; Col 2:19: "and not holding fast to the Head, from whom the whole body, nourished and knit together through its joints and ligaments, grows with a growth that is from God." We are baptized *eis Christon*, Rom 6:3; *eis hen sôma*, 1 Cor 12:13.
[17] Compare Col 1:24, "what is lacking. . . ."

143

Galen,[18] who had held that the sensitive and motor nerves of the entire body derived from the head. The head holds the whole body in unity, not only by the Spirit, within hearts, but also by the ministries which St. Paul describes as "gifts" made by the glorified Christ to equip the entire body and thus insure its growth (Eph 4:7–13). If the Head thus holds His body, the members will tend, in like manner, towards the Head, by means of all the joints and ligaments which the Head has arranged: Col 2:19 (in this verse, compared with the parallel text from Ephesians, it is possible to detect the difference in accent between the two letters: the Letter to the Colossians is more Christological, while the Letter to the Ephesians is more ecclesiological).

2. Christ, Invisible Leader of the Visible Church

A) HE IS TRULY THE LEADER

1. *The fact. Reality of His action*

On the subject of Christ, the New Testament uses words which express initiative: *archègos,* prince, leader of the people (Acts 3:15; 5:31), the one who founds and inaugurates a way of salvation (Heb 2:10; 12:2; compare *prodromos,* Heb 6:20). And, of course, all the expressions signifying His character of Shepherd, a shepherd who walks ahead, who does not wander off, but guides, and guides to pastures of life—;[19] first-fruits, first-born (1 Cor 15:20, 23; Rom 8:29; Heb 1:6; 2:10–18)—; *Aitios,* source, initiating cause of salvation. The idea of causality is also found, with the preposition *"dia,"* where the New Testa-

---

18 Cf. P. BENOIT, *op. cit.,* p. 133; S. TROMP, *op. cit.,* pp. 66–71.

19 Cf. Jn 10; 1 Pet 5:4. The first Christian centuries gave the theme of the Good Shepherd its full value: men are like a flock without a *logos* and are in need of the guidance of the *Logos:* cf. J. QUASTEN, "Der Gute Hirt in hellenistischer Logostheologie," in *Heilige Uberlieferung (Festgabe für I. Herwegen),* Münster, 1938, pp. 51–58.

ment speaks of the mediation of Jesus, of the blood of Jesus, or of His prayer, all of which obtain for us access to God and to salvation.

This character of leader is evidently confirmed in the area of example, and in an extremely profound way. We must pause here for a moment, for this is a very effective way indeed for Christ to be our Leader. What we suggest, for a better understanding of it, is that we take as our point of departure an idea which is a constant in the Christian tradition and which modern research induces us to reëvaluate: the idea of the unity of human nature. As individual persons, we are called, within the course of time, to participate in a single human nature. But we do not receive this nature merely as it is, limited to its pure essential definition, atemporally: the human nature which is communicated to us, which holds itself in readiness for our participation and personalization, is a human nature which has been enriched, developed, cultivated by centuries of history. For me, more particularly by the history of the West and, in fact, the little corner of the West which is bounded by the six sides of France.

Each person is capable of contributing something to this enriching of human nature. Those who do the most, and in the most obvious way, are the wise men, the geniuses, the heroes, and the saints: men who bypass the common measure, who project, beyond the line which has been reached and maintained by the great mass of men, ideas, examples, initiatives of such a nature that they attract others to themselves, in somewhat the same way as a commando or an elite troop attracts to itself an entire combat line which would otherwise be in danger of going stale.[20] In the humanity which I have received and which I have been asked to personalize, in the corner of the earth, in the moment of time in which I have been called to existence, I have actually been enriched by contributions which had become, at the very least,

[20] This is one of Bergson's themes in *The Two Sources of Morality and Religion,* New York, 1935.

possible determinations of human nature, and which were made
to me by Socrates, St. Augustine, Joan of Arc, Gandhi, Pascal,
and the rest. But over and above the greats—geniuses, heroes,
saints—there is the huge number of the little ones,[21] all the way
to our parents and our teachers, who, on a modest scale, have
accomplished the magnificent task of making man. . . .

Jesus, born of the Virgin Mary and of the Holy Spirit, enters
into this movement, the movement of humanity, at a precise
point in time and space. The contribution which He makes is
royal: non-Christians, non-believers acknowledge it; all men
agree that there is something of the absolute about the contribution of Jesus. For us, His disciples, this "something of the absolute" must be taken in the strictest sense of the term: in this
respect, first, that the contribution of Jesus Christ to human
nature is not limited to a particular determination of human life,
be it at the highest level, as for example courage, or tolerance,
or an appeal to conscience, for it touches the whole of human
life, its meaning pure and simple, its ultimate meaning. But
there is much more still. What Jesus Christ contributes to
humanity is not simply a *man's* determination. It is of course a
human one, one which He experienced and expressed in an
authentic human existence. But it is a determination which a
man contributes to humanity *when the man is God made man.*
It concerns the character of human nature as related to God,
where the relationship is one of image to model (Gen 1:26–27;
1 Cor 11:7). Man, though, is simply made *in* the image of God;
Christ is the Image of God. He, as Word and Son, is the Image
of God *in forma Dei.*[22] He, as Word or Son humanized, is the

[21] An example of this which is very close to us is the great number of
men who helped to make of twentieth-century Christians men of dialogue,
seeking fraternal unity in Christ; these were men like Charles Brent, Paul
Couturier, John Mott, and others.

[22] 2 Cor 4:4; Heb 1:2–3; Col 1:15. One of the most splendid efforts of
the theology of St. Thomas Aquinas was to show how the Word, in God, is
Son.

146

Image of God *in forma Servi.* He reveals, within a man's estate, the *true* image of God: "Philip, he who has seen me has seen the Father" (Jn 14:9). He reveals this image, quite precisely, *in forma servi,* and in doing this He not only *indicates* the way (Jn 14:6), but also effects a true theophany, the most sublime theophany prior to that of heaven.[23] At a given moment in time, under Caesar Augustus, Christ brought to humanity a new determination—the *absolute* determination. It concerned human nature taken in its relationship to its origin and its end, that is, to God, from whom it comes and to whom it is going. We would do well to recall here what was said above on the theme of *"plērōma,"* in connection with the theme of Christ-as-Leader.

Christ is thus the New Adam, restoring the heavenly image. For humanity, Christ is a new beginning: *Kephalē, Archē,* also, in that sense. And what He thus begins is the definitive man, the man of eternal life: the *Eschatos Adam* is the principle of eschatological humanity (cf. 1 Cor 15:45–49). Were we to say what this humanity is, we would have to outline a treatise on Christian anthropology. Let it suffice here to recall that the Church is the people made up of all who walk in the steps of the New and Last Adam towards the heritage of the Father, starting from the inaugural act of this progress: for Christ, His Pasch; for each Christian, his baptism, as Romans 6 bears out.[24]

Christ does not act solely as model or revealer. He is not Head, initiator, Principle, in the field of morality alone. When St. Thomas analyzes the way in which a man can act on another man, he makes a distinction between action by teaching or example and action by effective, organic or vital mode.[25] Max

[23] Cf. above, pp. 1f., "Christ, the Image of the Invisible God."

[24] The program was systematized in the theology of the Fathers, the Greek Fathers especially: cf. G. B. LADNER, *The Idea of Reform. Its Impact on Christian Thought and Action in the Age of the Fathers,* Cambridge (Mass.), 1959, pp. 85f.

[25] Cf. our Preface to G. F. VAN ACKEREN, *Sacra Doctrina . . . ,* Rome, 1952, and " 'Traditio' et 'Sacra Doctrina' chez saint Thomas d'Aquin," in *Eglise et Tradition,* edited by J. BETZ and H. FRIES, Le Puy and Lyons, 1963,

Scheler has shown, from another point of view, that there are two types of action which, frequently, are proper to different types of men: there are the patterns and there are the leaders.[26] Jesus Christ unites the two modes of action: He is leader and He is pattern. Better: He acts on the entire body of men, not only by teaching or example, but by vital movement and, initially, by an operation analogous to that of a begetter. Is not baptism compared to a second birth (Jn 3:3; Tit 3:5)?

Somehow or other, we shall have to lay hold of the notion that Christ acts effectively, not merely on the level of past historical facts, and originating in the Gospel and in the fact of salvation, but on the level of the present application of this salvation to all men. Tradition has expressed this idea in many ways. It has seen the glorified Christ as the High Priest intervening in a real way in each salvific act. Of this there are countless testimonies. As time went on, although this truth was neither denied nor disregarded, the subject of ever-greater detail came to be the role of the means of grace: the Church, the sacraments, the priesthood. St. Augustine, in attributing the sacramental acts *to Christ* as to their primary subject—"Peter baptizes, it is Christ who baptizes; Judas baptizes, it is Christ who baptizes"—had had in mind a basic truth. This attribution, however, was later invoked, against different opponents, in favor of the institution itself, and almost of an automatism in this institution. The sacramental *ex opere operato* which, properly understood, is an affirmation of the sovereignty of Christ's action has at times had its meaning distorted into one of automatism which it simply does not possess in authentic Catholic theology.

---

pp. 157–194 (pp. 162f.). It would be quite worthwhile to study the application of these categories throughout the theology of St. THOMAS AQUINAS. See, for example, IIIa, q. 69, a. 5.

[26] M. SCHELER, *Vorbilder und Führer* (first published in 1933); there is a French translation by E. MARNY, *Le Saint, le Génie, le Héros,* Lyons, 1958.

It is certainly true that guaranteed structures for the communication of the good things of the covenant exist. They are guaranteed, of course, in virtue of the will and gracious institution of God, but they are really guaranteed. The communication of the good things of the Covenant is not based on a pure *personal* relationship, nor on a pure occasionalism, a kind of dotted line of acts of God, acts free with the radical freedom of Grace.[27] Were we to think this, we would be misunderstanding these structures of the covenant, instituted by Grace incarnate. Still in all, there is, at the heart of these structures, a relationship in sanctifying grace which is always a personal relationship; and every spiritual gift, whether sanctifying grace or social charism, involves and accomplishes, viewed from the standpoint of God and of Christ, a purpose of immediately present grace.

2. Christ-as-Leader in the gift of grace. The Sacred Heart

It is obvious that we cannot identify Thomistic theology with Catholic dogma. We are, however, fully justified in following it, not out of servility and the spirit of conformity, but out of intellectual conviction and with great Christian joy, for it presents a picture of Christ with which our faith and spiritual experience find themselves wonderfully at ease. The Lord did indeed say: "Apart from me you can do nothing" (Jn 15:5); "No one comes to the Father, but by me" (Jn 14:6).

According to this theology, there is nothing holy, nothing good, which does not suppose, as instrumental cause, some act of the humanity assumed by the Son of God, a humanity which is body, sensitivity, spirit and will, knowledge and love. This theology makes it clear that the sacred humanity assumed by the

---

[27] Thus, the early Karl Barth (cf. J. HAMER, *Karl Barth,* Westminster, 1962). Compare Ruskin's question: "Who knows where it pleased God to let down his ladder?" But we *know* that it is in Jesus Christ, true Ladder of Jacob (Jn 1:51 = Gen 28:10–17), and in the entire mission which flows from His.

Word of God is an instrument, 1) which is not separated, as, for example, a hammer, a saw, or a bow, but *conjoined,* as is the hand; 2) which is *living,* moving itself, since intelligent and free.[28]

According to Thomistic theology, which had been fore-shadowed in that of St. John Damascene and, still earlier, in the Cappadocian Fathers and Cyril of Alexandria, every gift of grace which is made to men passes through the understanding and love of the Christ-man, and is perfectly in agreement with the divine Will: the Son knows the Father and always does His will. The Father, for His part, has constituted Christ in His character of Leader and Savior, and He effects the salvation of the world by associating to Himself, so that they might will it and effect it with Him, the soul, the intelligence, the love and the body of Jesus Christ, mediator between God and men. Thus it is that we receive no grace from God which does not presuppose and involve an act of Christ's knowledge and love for us: "The Son gives life to whom he will" (Jn 5:21).[29] This doctrine constitutes the firmest possible basis for devotion to the Sacred Heart, for this devotion is, fundamentally, nothing other than devotion to the "philanthropy of God" as it is made known in Jesus Christ.[30]

Biblically speaking, Jesus is the absolute Yes of all God's promises (2 Cor 1:20); He is the whole of God's plan of salvation for the entire world. Moses and the prophets, too, spoke

[28] The principal texts are: *Summa Theologiae,* IIIa, q. 7, a. 1, ad 3; q. 8, a. 1, ad 1; a. 5, ad 1; q. 18, a. 1, ad 2; q. 62, a. 5, especially ad 1; q. 64, a. 3 and a. 8; q. 69, a. 5; *De Veritate,* q. 29, a. 1, ad 9. Cf. I. BACKES, *Die Christologie des hl. Thomas v. Aq. und die Griechischen Kirchenväter,* Paderborn, 1931; Th. TSCHIPKE, *Die Menschheit Christi als Heilsorgan der Gottheit, unter bes. Berücksichtigung d. Lehre des hl. Thomas v. Aq.,* Freiburg, 1940; Cf.-V. HÉRIS, *Le mystère du Christ,* Paris, 1928.

[29] *"Gratia non derivatur a Christo in nos mediante natura humana, sed per solam personalem actionem ipsius Christi,"* IIIa, q. 8, a. 5, ad 1.

[30] Tit 3:4; cf. article referred to in note 23, *supra,* p. 25 especially; S. TROMP, *op. cit.,* pp. 88–89.

150

everywhere of Him. . . . In a humanity which is like to ours in all respects, save sin, He is constituted leader not only over the Church of the redeemed, but over the world as well. He is filled, from God, with all the energy and perfection corresponding to this mission (cf. our discussion of *plērōma,* above). Jesus Himself has opened and wholly offered His consciousness, His soul, His understanding, His will, His heart, and finally His body, so as to be perfectly what God wanted Him to be, namely, the minister and the leader of the world's salvation. The great principle by which St. Thomas was guided in the questions he devoted to the prerogatives and the weaknesses of our Lord was precisely this: Jesus received both sublime endowments and limitations, everything which was perfectly appropriate to His mission: "to bring many sons to glory" (Heb 2:10; compare 10:14), and even to restore meaning and life to all creation (Eph 1:10), but uniquely on the basis of the sacrifice of the cross.[31]

In virtue of this principle of the Christ-economy, St. Thomas attributed to Christ the perfection of knowledge which is necessary to the Saviour of the world (it being of course admitted that the soul of Christ was, for the divinity, an allied means, and this even as to its vitality and freedom of spirit), so as to introduce sinful men into the covenant of grace and to cause them to grow.[32] In the great Thomistic theology, the Eastern theme

[31] St. THOMAS AQUINAS, in *Tertia Pars,* enunciates this principle, in question 9 (for example, article 1: "*qua mediante* [natura humana Christi] *totum humanum genus ad perfectum erat adducendum*"; article 2, which cites Heb 2:10, as does Ia-IIae, q. 114, a. 6) and in q. 13, a. 2: "*Anima Christi, secundum quod est instrumentum Verbi sibi uniti, sic habuit instrumentalem virtutem ad omnes immutationes miraculosas faciendas,* ordinabiles ad Incarnationis finem, qui est instaurare omnia, sive quae in caelis, sive quae in terris sunt (Eph 1:10)."

[32] Cf. IIa, q. 9, a. 3. Christ is "Wisdom of God" (Col 2:3; 1 Cor 1:24 and 30). Modern exegetes have drawn attention to the transfer to Christ of the Old Testament Wisdom theology: cf. H. WINDISCH, "Die Göttliche Weisheit der Juden und die paulinische Christologie," in *Neutestl. Studien für G. Heinrici,* Leipzig, 1914, pp. 220–234 (survey of the state of the ques-

151

of the assumption by God of a concrete humanity, and the Western scholastic theme of capital grace converge.

3. *The Church is built from and in heaven*

"Blessed be the God and Father of our Lord Jesus Christ, who has blessed us and filled us with every spiritual benefit in the heavens, in Christ" (Eph 1:3). "In Christ" signifies the causality of Christ in the execution of the Design of grace: the preposition *"en"* is rich in meaning, but we would be making a mistake if we were to put the emphasis on a signification of place. Its principal value is this: starting from Christ, in dependence on Him, Christ being the principle of the new creation. The preposition expresses His mediation and His instrumentality, all the while connoting, however, a mode of union, almost of interiority, with regard to this causality.

The design of grace does have a proper "place": heaven. Our Leader is there: Eph 1:20; 2:6; Col 3:1. From there He builds His body beginning with His Pasch—death-resurrection-being seated in the heavenly places—to which baptism unites us: Rom 6:3–11; Col 1:12; 2:12; 3:1–4; Eph 2:6; 5:26–27. The ecclesial body of Christ is established on earth, by means of bodily mediations which put our bodies, that is, our whole persons, into contact with the paschal body of Jesus Christ, but it is built in heaven.[33] "Our life is hidden with Christ in God" (Col 3:3).

---

tion); C. F. BURNEY, *Christ as ARXH of Creation*, in *JTS*, 1926, pp. 160–177; B. BOTTE, "La Sagesse et les origines de la Christologie," in *Rev. Sc. phil. théol.*, 21 (1932), pp. 54–67; and especially A. FEUILLET, cited *supra*, note 8; compare H. SCHLIER in *Die Kirche nach dem Epheserbrief* (FT *Le Temps de l'Eglise*, Tournai-Paris, 1961, p. 170 and n. 1; pp. 180–181).

[33] Heaven is the place, both spiritual and corporeal, where God is fully God for and in His creature, where God is truly "everything to everyone" (1 Cor 15:28) and is known as such: cf. *The Wide World, My Parish*, Baltimore, 1961, pp. 44–61; 70–83. The means God uses to pursue His design to be everything to everyone is Christ fulfilled in the *plērōma*, that is, the being-according-to-God, the being filled with the Sovereign Presence of

The body grows towards its heavenly Head and strives to equal the fullness of its leader: Eph 2:15; 4:12, 15; compare Phil 3:14.

Thus, the Church is in the world, functioning within it through sensible, visible means, particularly the sacraments. But what the Church does there is not of the world. It comes from on high and is leading on high. Within the world's cosmic and historical time, the Church lives her own history. It is the history of grace, the history of participation in the Fullness of Christ which her leader gives her from heaven, from the perfect Presence and Sovereignty of God, so as to lead the world back to this Presence and Sovereignty. It is a history of the "missions" of grace, in the sense intended by St. Thomas, *Ia Pars*, q. 43, a history of holiness. Its term is "the perfect Man, in all the strength of maturity, who realizes the fullness of Christ" (Eph 4:13, 15–16). But, divine and transcendent though it be, this history is not unrelated to secular history. For, as Christ came "for us and for our salvation," His gifts are freely made in response to the needs of the world, and most particularly in response to the new developments which are made in the course of time by mankind and the energies it draws from the cosmos.

B) CHRIST IS THE INVISIBLE LEADER OF THE VISIBLE CHURCH

Why invisible? "Invisible" is traditionally an attribute of "God," that is to say, of the Father, Source of the divinity;[34] but Christ is His image (Col 1:15), the one in whom and by whom He becomes manifest (Jn 1:18; 14:9) or will so become (1 Tim

---

God (Col 2:9). He re-conforms the world according to this being by first forming for Himself a body, the Church, through which He attracts everything else to Himself (Jn 12:32).

[34] Col 1:15; Jn 1:18; 1 Tim 1:17; 6:16. There are many ancient creeds which give *invisibilis* as an attribute of the Father: cf. A. HAHN, *Bibliothek der Symbole und Glaubensregeln der alten Kirche*, Breslau, 1897 (Index, under *Invisibilis*).

6:14–16). The function of revealing the Father is, in fact, one of His attributes (cf. *supra,* note 23). If Christ is at present invisible, He is invisible as to us and in relationship to our condition, for He is the principle of a creation *other* than the present. Ours is the creation of the flesh, but Christ is dead according to the flesh, inasmuch as He was born of a woman, born under the Law (Gal 4:4). Risen according to the Spirit, He has become life-giving Spirit (1 Cor 15:45), and it is as such that He is effectively our Leader, the Last Adam, the Principle of a new existence for the world. Such is the position of Him whose Pasch is achieved.

Ours is not, but is solely on the way to its achievement. This is why, from one point of view, we are already in the final "eon,"[35] why we are already involved in the eschatological: we already have the Spirit,[36] and St. Paul goes so far as to say that we are already seated in heaven (Eph 2:6). But we have only the pledge of the Spirit, and this is not enough to transform our entire being.[37] So that if Christ is "life-giving Spirit," His action must still be received at present in "psychic" and even "carnal" men. That is "carnal" which is of *this* creation: the natural being, neutral, even good in itself, but of itself weak and perishable; the earthly being in its condition of subjection and of inclination to sin.[38] The being of which we speak possesses its own form of existence, but it is inclined to ignorance of anything other than itself, not knowing from whom it comes and for whom it is

[35] Cf. Acts 2:17; Eph 1:10, and all the statements on the *kainōtēs.*
[36] Col 1:12–13; Eph 1:14; 2:18–22; Rom 8:14–17.
[37] Cf. 2 Cor 1:22; 5:5; Eph 1:14; Rom 8:18–25.
[38] Because of this situation, St. Paul says sometimes that we have put off the body of flesh (in baptism, namely, in the measure in which Christ lives in us), sometimes that we, though living in the flesh, should nevertheless not live according to the flesh, but should mortify its doings; cf., e.g., 2 Cor 10:2f. See W. SCHAUF, *Sarx . . . ,* Munich, 1924; W. GRUTHOD, *Die paulinische Anthropologie,* Stuttgart, 1934; P. VAN IMSCHOOT, in *Encyclopedic Dictionary of the Bible,* New York, 1963, cols. 259–261.

made: for it, there is no correlation which must be sought between its form and its end, what it is and what it is for; it is content to enjoy *its* being. From one standpoint, it runs the risk of not giving glory to its Creator (compare Rom 1:18f.) and of "taking glory" in itself;[39] from another standpoint, of failing to realize the *meaning* of its existence as an *existence-according-to-God,* penetrated by His Presence, and thus destined to share His Glory.[40]

The Church is not in all respects immune from the weaknesses and temptations of the flesh. Made up of men who live in the flesh, she is not totally penetrated and transformed by the Spirit. With them, by them, she still dwells in the "*regio dissimilitudinis*" of which we read in St. Augustine and in the spiritual tradition of like inspiration.[41] To be sure, the Church, as a creative whole and as a collective person, more exactly as the Spouse of Christ, has promises of indefectibility which the faithful, taken individually, do not have. But these promises exonerate her neither from all temptation nor from all weakness. They guarantee her that the powers of death will not prevail against her, not that she will be unaffected by weakness. We need only read the letters of St. Paul to the community at Corinth, his warnings to the faithful in "Asia" (Eph 4:20–24), the letters to the Churches

---

[39] The *kaukhasthaï,* the *kaukhēsis,* of which St. Paul so often speaks, and which is the act of one who does not know that God is the source of all and for all: cf., e.g., 1 Cor 1:26–31 and 8:6; BULTMANN, *TWNT,* vol. III, pp. 646–654.

[40] We saw above the relationship of this with Christ's role as *kephalē* and with the *plērōma.* For one form of existence, salvation consists in realizing its meaning, its end; and, realizing this perfectly through the sovereign and glorious Presence of "God everything in everyone," to give thanks for it. Hell consists in maintaining one's existence when one has lost the meaning of existence and suffers a bitter and despairing remorse because of the fact: cf. *The Wide World, My Parish,* Baltimore, 1961, pp. 70–83.

[41] St. AUGUSTINE, *Confess.,* VII, 10, 16; cf. Etienne GILSON, " 'Regio dissimilitudinis' de Platon à saint Bernard de Clairvaux," in *Mediaeval Studies,* 9 (1947), pp. 108f.; G. DUMEIGE, article "Dissemblance," in *Dictionnaire de Spiritualité,* vol. III, cols. 1330f.

of the Apocalypse, in order to see what the situation was during the lifetime of the apostles.

One of the most characteristic features of the ecclesiology of the Fathers and of the liturgy is the fact that it embraces anthropology. Their Church is very actively viewed as made up of men. They apply to it the New Testament themes of Christian anthropology concerning redeemed man, the struggle of the spirit against the flesh. They apply to it the images and types in which the Bible expressed man's situation and the situation of the people of God in the face of sin, and under the influence of Grace (types such as Rahab, Mary Magdalen, etc.). It followed from this that a certain tension remained between the Church and the Church's Lord, between the historical condition of the Church and her ideal type, whose sublime image the Fathers and the liturgy never ceased to sketch.

Since the medieval era, we have more or less passed over to a predominant assertion of the conformity of the Church to her ideal type and of an adequation of what is done by her and what is done by Jesus Christ. This process has followed two routes which have ended up by converging. On the one hand, there has been the development of the juridical consideration of the privileges of the Church and of priestly authority. This development is particularly noticeable beginning with the latter part of the eleventh century (the Hildebrandine reform and its sequels). On the other hand, there has been the development of an organic conception of the Church as the body of Christ in a biological sense. This conception has asserted itself in various historical contexts, in certain medieval statements on the mystical body in connection with the theology of capital grace and with corporative ideology, and then in certain romantic descriptions of the Church as an organism. We have witnessed a particular fondness for St. Augustine's formula, "the whole Christ," or for the formula of St. Joan of Arc, "I think that between our Lord and the Church—it is all one," or Bossuet's "The Church is Jesus

Christ spread forth and communicated," or for the theme of "continuing incarnation."[42]

Many of the texts and themes which express the intimate relationship between Christ and the Church might well be understood either in the sense of an identification, tending to absolutize the institution, or in a sense which would preserve the affirmation of the transcendence of Christ. Take, for example, the beautiful text from Saint Cyprian: "Christ, whose sovereign will, present to His Church and to her leaders, governs both."[43] We could perfectly well take this as a reference to a hierarchy which absolutely incorporates the action of Christ, or we could insist on the sovereignty and the actuality of Christ's action. . . . The development of ideas has moved principally in the former sense. The two routes, the juridical and the organic-mystical, have converged. The juridical acquires its full force when it is carried along by a mystique. The juridical elements in the institution have been viewed, in the mystical light of the organism, as representing, or, rather, as being the very organs *of Christ:*[44] what He is, but not purely and simply, nor without involving other aspects as well. The Church is not physically the mouth of Christ, the Church is *His envoy.* . . . To be sure, the Church does bear the mediation of salvation, but only as a minister of the sovereign action of Christ. Between the Church and Christ, this difference exists: in Christ, the characteristics of minister of salvation and of source or principle (Head) overlap, while the Church is not the principle. Some distance still remains between the characteristic of mediatrix or sacrament and the Head who infuses her with life.

---

[42] An example of this type of presentation is R. H. BENSON, *Christ in the Church,* St. Louis, 1911.

[43] "[*Christum*] *qui arbitrio et nutu ac praesentia et praepositos ipsos et ecclesiam cum praepositis gubernat . . . ,*" *Epist.* 66, 9, 1.

[44] A quite representative example of this approach (there are others which are still bolder!) is P. CHARLES, "Vicarius Christi," in *NRT,* 1929, pp. 443–459 (reprinted in *L'Eglise, sacrement du monde,* Paris-Bruges, 1960, pp. 111–117).

To view the relationship between the Church and Christ in no other way than within the framework of an organism which would embrace both, as if there were a relationship of identity on the level of life and activity, and to quote only those scriptural texts which speak in such fashion, is to risk not giving credit to other scriptural assertions, which are assertions of duality and tension.

A duality in terms exists. The relationship between the Church and Christ is not of the substantial-organic type, but of the personal type. It is precisely in the letter said to be to the Ephesians, where the new understanding of the mystery, received by Paul in captivity, most especially undergoes ecclesiological development, that the Apostle attributes to the Church a kind of autonomy, proper to a moral person, before Christ, who was constituted as her Leader, above her:

> He has put all things under his feet and has made him the head over all things for the church, which is his body (1:22–23).
>
> Rather, speaking the truth in love, we are to grow up in every way into him who is the head, into Christ, from whom the whole body . . . (4:15–16).
>
> For the husband is the head of the wife as Christ is the head of the church, his body, and is himself its Savior. As the church is subject to Christ, so let wives also be subject in everything to their husbands. Husbands, love your wives, as Christ loved the church and gave himself up for her, that he might sanctify her, having cleansed her by the washing of water with the word, that he might present the church to himself in splendor, without spot or wrinkle or any such thing, that she might be holy and without blemish (5:23–27).

Unfortunately, this theme of Church-as-spouse was very early —and particularly after St. Augustine—interpreted in the light of the verses which follow, that is, under the sign and in the sense of the *una caro*,[45] and thus there was a return to identifica-

---

[45] Cf. Claude CHAVASSE, *The Bride of Christ. An Enquiry into the Nuptial Element in Early Christianity*, London, n.d. (1939). It is evident, in St. Augustine, that the theme of *una caro* is ceaselessly linked with that of *Christus integer, unus homo*, with resonances of texts like Acts 9:4.

158

tion. The full truth of the dualism which is implied in the personal relationship has been somewhat swallowed up in the assertion of organic unity. Among the Fathers and among the medieval theologians, there were themes which compensated for this, and in which the duality, even the tension, were strongly brought out. The Fathers, for example, had the curious—though extremely rich and imbued with a profound ecclesiology—theme of the *mysterium lunae*.[46] During the Middle Ages, there was the vitality of the idea of the Church as *congregatio fidelium,* the ensemble and corporation of Christians, thus a distinct collective person. . . . In her prayerful and liturgical action, the Church is both closely united to her Lord, and constituted before Him as His spouse. . . .

One aspect of the life of the Church has been the struggle to preserve the spirit of Christ, and this is not expressed by the idea of an organism whose life, purely and simply, is the life of Christ. If St. Paul so often made use of military or athletic metaphors, it was not simply because these were elements of the ordinary framework of life, nor for some rhetorical end. He used them because they well expressed the tension of Christian life. A certain tension, a certain dialogue, are integral to the militant condition of the Church. The Church must *tend towards* equality with her Leader (Eph 4:15), and this can be done only by seeking to be subject to Him as a wife is to her husband. To the extent that the Church, as the Fathers saw her, and as the liturgy and a liberal theological tradition have seen her, is made up of men, of the baptized, a constant tension can be perceived within her, deriving from the effort to convert the nominally, the super-

---

[46] On this point, cf. Hugo RAHNER, "Mysterium lunae. Ein Beitrag zur Kirchentheologie der Väterzeit," in *Zeitschrift für kath. Theologie,* 63 (1939), pp. 311–349, 428–442; 64 (1940), pp. 61–80, 121–131 (cf. "The Mystery of the Moon," in *Greek Myths and Christian Mystery,* London, 1963, pp. 154–176). What was involved was the posing of two stars, one having light only from the other, and undergoing besides phases of increase and decrease.

ficially, the sinfully Christian to a real, serious, and pure Christian life:[47] in short, from the effort to retain intact the seal of baptism and to be, eschatologically, what we have been made in baptism, men "sanctified and cleansed by the washing of water with the word" (Eph 5:26).

It would be easy to outline an application of these considerations to several problems which are always being discussed. We will allude to three of them, without pretending to do anything more than pose questions along the lines of the preceding explanations.

a) *Dogmatic knowledge.* It is generally recognized that St. Thomas emphasizes the fact that dogmatic formulas are neither the term nor the object of the knowledge of faith, but are merely the means in which and through which the mind can approach the reality of the very mystery which is the object of its adherence: "*Assensus fidei* [or *Actus credentis*] *non terminatur ad enuntiabile, sed ad rem.*"[48] Among the definitions of the "*articulus fidei,*" that is, of dogma, he retains a formula, attributed to St. Isidore, which holds that dogma represents a perception of salvific truth which leaves the mind of the believer more or less unsatisfied, however much he strains towards the real perception of the Truth itself: "*Perceptio veritatis tendens in ipsam.*"[49]

[47] In an ecclesiology in which the idea that the Church is made up of Christians was operative, the "without spot or wrinkle" of Eph 5:27 was often explained by a greater or lesser *approach* to perfect Christianity, depending on the faithful. Cf. H. RIEDLINGER, *Die Makellosigkeit der Kirche in den lateinischen Hoheliedkommentaren des Mittelalters,* Münster, 1958.

[48] *Summa Theologiae,* IIa-IIae, q. 1, a. 2, ad 2; *De Veritate,* q. 14, a. 8, ad 5. Cf. M.-D. CHENU, "L'unité de la foi," in *La Vie Spirituelle, Suppl.,* July, 1937, pp. 1–8; M.-L. GUÉRARD DES LAURIERS, *Dimensions de la foi,* Paris, 1952, vol. I, pp. 169–170, 328.

[49] *In III Sent.,* d. 25, q. 1, a. 1, q. 1, obj. 4; *Summa Theologiae,* IIa-IIae, q. 1, a. 6, *sed contra.* The formula's author is, perhaps, William of Auxerre. See J. M. PARENT, "La notion de dogme au XIIIe siècle," in *Et. d'Hist. litt. et doctr. du XIIIe siècle,* Paris, 1932, vol. I, pp. 141–163.

CHRIST, INVISIBLE LEADER OF THE VISIBLE CHURCH

This supposes, in the earthly conditions of our grasp of the mysteries of faith, a situation consonant with that of the entire Church striving to "grow into the head" (Eph 4:15; compare "to be baptized *into* Christ," Rom 6:3; 1 Cor 12:12).

b) When we study the present confrontation of *Catholic teaching* and *Protestant theology* on the question of tradition, we see that considerable progress has been made since the sixteenth century, even since the beginning of the twentieth, but that very serious reasons for disagreement still exist. The progress has consisted in this: whereas the first Reformers of the sixteenth century did not at first distinguish between tradition and traditions, and indiscriminately attacked the whole in a purely negative or critical way, contemporary Protestant theologians make a distinction between tradition and traditions; recognizing the place of the latter, they affirm the value of the former, in respect of Scripture itself, in truly positive fashion. The principal disagreement goes to the question of whether tradition has a *proper* normative value, or only a derivative value, stemming from Scripture by reason of its conformity with it. But this question itself has repercussions on the question of the relationship between tradition and the Church or, more precisely still, the magisterium of the Church, if such magisterium exists.

Since the sixteenth century, but especially since the last, Catholic theology has more and more distinctly tended to insist on the role of the magisterium as *constitutive* of tradition, not in its documentary materiality, but in its formality as ecclesiastical norm of belief. It has unwearyingly accounted for the value of tradition by the active presence of the Holy Spirit which has been given to the Church and does not cease to assist her. This line of thought is, as a matter of fact, as old as the Church herself, but it has been developed since the middle ages, in the West, to the point of being held sufficient to justify adherence to a point of doctrine, held by the Church as being of faith, independently of

161

scriptural attestation or even of ancient documentation. Ultimately, it was in just this way that Pius XII supported the declaration of the bodily assumption of the Mother of God as a dogma
of faith.[50]

Protestants criticize these positions on the basis of considerations which vary somewhat in their formulation, but amount to
saying this:[51] to hold these positions would be to identify the
Church with her norm, and then to make of the Church the
norm itself, instead of subjecting her to the norm of the Word of
God. It would take away from the Church a *"Gegenüber,"* a *vis-
à-vis,* and so suppress the duality as really to admit a relationship
of identity. Under such conditions, says Karl Barth, the Church
would only be in monologue with herself. Protestant theology
seeks to preserve the dualist and personal relationship of a
Church which *can* be unfaithful, but which strives to be faithful,
with her Lord made manifest or present in His Word which
unceasingly judges the Church.

[50] For the history of this, see *La Tradition et les traditions,* I. *Essai his-
torique,* Paris, 1960, chs. III to VI.

[51] We are referring particularly to K. BARTH, *Die Schrift und die Kirche*
(Theol. Studien, 22), Zürich, 1947; *Church Dogmatics,* vol. 1, Part 2, New
York, 1956, pp. 538f.; O. CULLMANN, *The Early Church. Historical and
Theological Studies,* London, pp. 57–99; K. E. SKYDSGAARD, "Scripture and
Tradition. Remarks on the Problem of Tradition in Theology Today," in
The Scottish Journal of Theology, 9 (1956), pp. 337–358 (cf. pp. 344f.);
E. KINDER, "Schrift und Tradition," in *Begegnung der Christen. Festgabe
für Otto Karrer,* Einsiedeln, 1959, pp. 115–131 (cf. pp. 118–119 and 129);
H. ENGELLAND, "Schrift und Tradition," in *Theol. Literaturzeitung,* 85
(1960), cols. 19–32 (cf. 28–29); compare H. DIEM, quoted in *Istina,* 3
(1956), p. 401. And cf. P. LENGSFELD, *Ueberlieferung. Tradition und
Schrift in der evangelischen-kathol. Theol. der Gegenwart,* Paderborn, 1960,
p. 186. The objection made to us goes beyond the question of tradition but,
under one form or another, remains always the same: the Catholic Church
believes that it adequately embodies in itself the work of God or His action.
It thus tends to identify itself with the Kingdom of God and with its proper
norm. See, for example, H. VON LOEWENICH, *Der moderne Katholizismus,*
Witten, 1955; K. G. STECK, "Das Selbstverständnis der Römischen Kirche,"
in *Evangelische Theologie,* 15 (1955); R. MEHL, *Du Catholicisme romain.
Approche et interprétation,* Neuchâtel-Paris, 1957; F. J. LEENHARDT,
Catholicisme romain et Protestantisme, Genève, 1957.

There is more than one Protestant theologian who sees as the source of what seems to him a deviation, the great Roman Catholic deviation, an interpretation of the Church-as-body-of-Christ which is along the lines of biological identity with Christ.[52] Other points where Protestant opposition stems from the same difference might be cited. Thus: the relationship between "Church" and "Kingdom of God"; the way of conceiving the marks of the Church, unity, catholicity, apostolicity, holiness; the idea of a possible "breach of trust" and of a penitence *of the Church* as such. . . . What we have here are so many articles where the Protestant position is based on the desire to preserve a tension between the Church and her ideal limit. Protestant theology seeks always to maintain the latter *in God* and not to invest it or make it immanent in the Church herself, even though it were by a gracious gift of God.

There are quite a few criticisms which we could make of Protestant theology. It seems to us to fail to recognize the full reality of the gift of God, the truth of the relationship between the Infinite and the finite, eternity and time, the Giver and His gift. But this is not the sort of thing that can be said in a few words. What we intended was simply to situate, in relation to the theme we have discussed, a question which the Reform addresses to us. It is a very great question indeed, and we must not expect to put ourselves right in its regard at too small a cost.

c) The question of *the members of the Church*. Since the solemn declarations of the encyclical *Mystici Corporis* of June 29th, 1943, articles and studies have not ceased to appear on this problem—the sign of a certain dissatisfaction, of difficulties which have not been resolved. We know that the encyclical affirmed: 1) the identity between the "mystical body" of Christ

[52] Cf., e.g., G. EBELING, *Kirchengeschichte als Geschichte der Auslegung der Heiligen Schrift*, Tübingen, 1947, p. 17; P. BONNARD, cited *supra,* note 1 (without application to tradition).

163

and the Roman Catholic Church: the body of Christ, in fact, is not merely the domain of the spiritual action of Christ (something which could be believed solely by following the line of thought of the *Christological* treatise of IIIa, q. 8, a. 3); it is the organized social body of which Christ is the Head by reason of a number of relationships, developed in the papal document. 2) Consequently, only the members of the Roman Catholic Church can truly be called members of the mystical body of Christ. To the extent that others have been graced with spiritual gifts, namely, informed faith and supernatural justice, they are simply said to have been "ordered to the mystical body."

The dissatisfaction which is often expressed stems, we think, from the fact that, in spite of everything, "body *of Christ*" does not say exactly the same things as "Church." The two expressions point to the same subject, but they do not speak about it in exactly the same way, nor, undoubtedly, on the same level. Christ-as-Leader is invisible, whereas the Church is visible. Christ is a transcendent principle, whereas the Church is a defined and ascertainable organism on earth. The action of Christ reaches to the interior, to the plane of one's personal moral attitude towards God; the Church "*de internis non judicat,*" she reaches what is socially accessible, counting among her members some men who are not truly of Christ, while ignoring others who are. How does the action of the two overlap? Should we not expect that the action of the one would be more extensive or more restricted than the action of the other? The field of Christ's influence and that of the Church's will converge eschatologically, when "*quidquid latet apparebit*" and the real and the invisible will coalesce. There can be no question that, if we reserve the title of "[mystical] Body" to the visible and organized ecclesial institution, we must speak as the encyclical does. But what title are we to give to the field in which Christ really acts, although there is no external adherence to His visible ecclesial Body? We could, of course, refuse to suggest "mystical body" because, in St. Paul,

164

"body of Christ" implies a bodily communion in the body of Jesus, through baptism and the Eucharist. But is it not as their leader that Christ acts on these men? And not merely in the way He can act on the cosmos or on the Powers, whose Leader St. Paul well says He is, without, for all that, calling them His body. For it is salvific gifts which are involved here, and, from the standpoint of men, possibly a true obedience in faith and a true love, even though psychologically unconscious. If we look at the question from the standpoint of the action *of Christ,* how shall we name the bond which His action creates between such men and Him? We can imagine other expressions: communion of saints, society of the called, the saved. . . . But all of this reveals the tension which exists between the visible ecclesial body and its invisible Leader.

The Church *tends* towards an adequate convergence with the salvific action of her Leader: *in intensity,* that is, by bringing her response of faithfulness and fervor up to the level which her Leader expects of her, through internal reform, through the effort to purify herself, to present herself to Him "without spot or wrinkle." Pope John XXIII used this phrase more than once when speaking of the task assigned to the Second Vatican Council; —*in extension,* with regard to potential or imperfect members of the body of Christ, whom the Church wishes to incorporate fully into the body of Christ which she is, and in which the Lord has set forth the good things of the covenant and the means of salvation, in all their purity and plenitude. This activity is also divided into two parts, depending on whether the question is one of potential or imperfect members who are strangers to every positive institution of Christian salvation (this is mission in the strict meaning of the word), or one of imperfect members who already participate in at least some of the goods of the covenant: Jews (Old Testament), separated Christians (and here it is ecumenism which is involved).

165

Reform, mission, ecumenism: so many activities essential to the Church inasmuch as she is, in the sense we have attempted to make more precise, the visible and earthly body of her invisible and heavenly Leader.

2

The Lordship of Christ
over the Church and over the World[1]

1. *The Lordship of Christ.* 1. The lordship of Christ is total and absolute. 2. The full effective exercise of the lordship of Christ is eschatological. Its term is the realization of perfect monotheism. 3. The "economic" exercise (the earthly administration of the redemption) of His lordship by Christ includes a

[1] Report edited in behalf of the "*Conférence catholique pour les questions oecuméniques,*" and by no means without making use of the many useful observations which were made on a first draft by members of the *Conférence.* It is reproduced here with the authorization of its secretary, J. Willebrands. It was first published in *Istina,* 1959, pp. 131–166. What follows is a bibliographical sketch, evidently incomplete, of Catholic studies on the lordship of Christ: Scripture, and syntheses of scriptural inspiration: L. CERFAUX, articles beginning in 1922, reprinted in *Recueil Lucien Cerfaux,* 2 vols., Gembloux, 1954; B. RIGAUX, *L'Antéchrist et l'opposition au Royaume messianique dans l'Ancien et le Nouveau Testament,* Gembloux-Paris, 1932; Fr. MUSSNER, *Christus, das All und die Kirche,* Trier, 1955; J. BONSIRVEN, *Le Règne de Dieu,* Paris, 1957; E. DRINKWELDER, *Vollendung in Christus,* Paderborn, 1934; Th. MICHELS, *Das Heilswerk der Kirche. Ein Beitrag z. einer Theol. d. Geschichte,* Salzburg-Leipzig, 1935; O. BAUHOFER, *Die Heimholung der Welt,* Freiburg, 1936; J. CASPER, *Weltverklärung im liturgischen Geiste der Ostkirche,* Freiburg, 1939 (compare H. Urs VON BALTHASAR, *Kosmische Liturgie. Maximus der Bekenner,* Freiburg, 1941); H. BIEDERMANN, *Die Erlösung der Schöpfung beim Apostel Paulus,* Würzburg, 1940; J. PINSK, *Hoffnung auf Herrlichkeit,* Colmar, n.d. (1942); G. THILS, *Théologie des Réalités terrestres . . . ,* vol. I, Paris, 1947; E. WALTER, *Christus und der Kosmos,* Stuttgart, 1948. And cf. the various works on "theology of history."

Tradition, magisterium, history: E. SCHARL, *Recapitulatio Mundi,* Freiburg, 1941 (St. Irenaeus); E. STAEHELIN, *Die Verkündigung des Reiches Gottes in der Kirche Jesu Christi. Zeugnisse aus allen Jahrhunderten und*

duality of domains, Church and world, a struggle (the resistance of the Powers and of the flesh), and, in Christ Himself, a priestly mode of suffering Servant.

2. *The Lordship of Christ over the Church.*

3. *The Exercise of the Lordship of Christ over the World.* 1. The lordship of Christ over the world being exercised within the creational structures of the world. 2. The lordship of Christ being exercised over the world by the Church. Addendum.

1. The Lordship of Christ

By the faith which corresponds to the apostolic word, we hold truths about the lordship of Christ which Christian experience tries to translate, but which greatly surpass that experience. "Jesus is *Kyrios*." This, though without excluding other formulas or other affirmations, was the profession of faith of Christians, the apostles and then the witnesses who were made "martyrs" by this very affirmation, when pushed to its consequences of rejection of all idolatry.[2]

---

allen Konfessionen, 4 vols., Basel, 1951–1958 (The author is Protestant. Annotated translations of texts. Review by J. Leclercq in *Rev. Hist. ecclés.,* 53 [1958], pp. 57–68); J. LECLERCQ, *L'idée de la Royauté du Christ au Moyen Age,* Paris, 1959; PIUS XI, encyclical *Quas Primas, AAS,* 17 (1925), pp. 593f.; PIUS XII, encyclical *Summi Pontificatus,* October 20th, 1939, *AAS,* 31 (1939), pp. 413f., and cf. *infra,* note 69.

Systematic theology: Ed. HUGON "La fête spéciale de Jésus-Christ Roi," in *Revue thomiste,* 30 (1925), pp. 297–320; Ch.-V. HÉRIS, "La Royauté du Christ," in *Rev. Sc. phil. théol.,* 15 (1926), pp. 297–324 (reprinted in *Le Mystère du Christ,* Paris, 1928, pp. 148f.); L. CHAMBAT, *La Royauté du Christ selon la doctrine catholique,* Paris, 1931; M.-J. NICOLAS, "Le Christ, Roi des nations," in *Revue thomiste,* 44 (1938), pp. 437–481; H. BOUESSÉ, *Un seul Chef ou Jésus-Christ Chef de l'univers et Tête des saints,* Paris, 1950; M. THIEL, "Anteil der vernunftlosen Geschöpfe an der Gottesverherr-lichung des Menschen," in *Divus Thomas,* 1952, pp. 185–200.

Spirituality and popularization: D. DE MONLÉON, *Le Christ-Roi,* Paris, 1933; A. TAINIER, *Jésus notre Roi,* Paris-Louvain, 1934; L. DEIMEL, *Das Reich Gottes,* Wiesbaden, 1935.

[2] See O. CULLMANN, *The Earliest Christian Confessions,* London, 1949. —Idea of the kingship of Christ, His imperial character, among the martyrs of the first three centuries: references in *Recueil Lucien Cerfaux,* vol. I, pp.

At the origin of this affirmation we find full monotheism, consistent monotheism, the monotheism which was the soul of Israel: "Hear, O Israel: The Lord our God is one Lord."[3] This full monotheism brings with it two principal consequences:

1. Everything is God's. Things are not *truly*, they are not good and true except when, conformed to the creative Word of God, they realize His will and His plan.[4] What is more, everything which God has made is good. "God did not make death, and he does not delight in the death of the living. For he created all things that they might exist."[5] Seeing the entire universe as dependent on God and on His design, revelation is a stranger to the modern opposition between "nature" and "spirit." Revelation knows but one creation, in which things and men are interdependent.

2. Yahweh is Lord. In this formula,[6] the theology of the Old Testament can be all the better summed up, in that the Old Testament reveals little about the nature of God in Himself; in point of fact, it does not otherwise reveal it, for it is concerned, from one end to the other, with telling us what God is for man and what man becomes in accordance with his relationship with God. Yahweh is He who rules all things, He whose desires must

---

31 f.; the Acts of the Martyrs are dated "under the reign of our Lord Jesus Christ, to whom glory . . ." (*ibid.*, p. 56). The same note, in modern form, is to be found among the martyrs of the Calles persecutions in Mexico, July, 1926 and after: F. DE LANVERSIN, "Témoins du Christ-Roi," in *La Vie Spirituelle*, March, 1928, pp. 742, 756; V. MARMOITON, *Apôtre et martyr, le P. Pro* (1891–1927), Toulouse, 1953. And, of course, the witnesses of the Confessing Church, under Hitler.

[3] Deut 6:4; compare 4:35; 32:39; Ex 10:1–3; Is 44:6; Mk 12:27–32; 1 Cor 8:4.

[4] Cf., e.g., Deut 32:39; Jer 2:13; 17:5–8, and see Claude TRESMONTANT, *A Study of Hebrew Thought*, New York, 1960; *Etudes de métaphysique biblique*, Paris, 1955; Th. BOMAN, *Hebrew Thought Compared with Greek*, Philadelphia, 1960.

[5] Wis 1:13–14; cf. Gen 1:31; Sir 39:2–35 (Vulgate, 26–41); 1 Tim 4:4.

[6] Cf. L. KOEHLER, *Theologie des Alten Testaments*, Tübingen, 3d ed., 1953; M. BUBER, *Das Königtum Gottes*, Heidelberg, 3d ed., 1956.

be followed, He whose government leads to life. And He *alone* is the Lord. The prophets developed this affirmation in a way which went beyond the mere granting of a human kingship which at first dissatisfied God but was later, in David, blessed by Him; the prophets were to make of it the type of kingship of the Messiah. The post-exilic restoration endeavored to realize this ideal of a kingship of Yahweh alone (theocracy). But Israel is no more the exclusive domain of the kingship of Yahweh than man, in creation, is isolated from the world. The sovereignty of God has for its domain all peoples, and it subjects their history to its designs. The only difference is that the others obey without knowing it, while Israel is called to a subjection of itself from the heart and to a witnessing of what God wills to be for us. It thus becomes, as the people of God, "a kingdom of priests and a holy nation" (Ex 19:5–6; 1 Pet 2:5, 9–10). The kingship of Yahweh thus converges with His character as Creator: it leads creation to its goal. The purpose of consistent monotheism is that Creation be accomplished through the reign. Isaiah, who announces to Zion, "Your King reigns," links this kingship of God with His status as Creator (40:21–26; 42:5). Several of the "kingship psalms" (cf. Ps 93; 96) do the same. With the prophets, promises of cosmic restoration are linked to the realization of messianic justice, that is, subjection to the reign of God.[7]

In more than a hundred New Testament passages,[8] in express or implicit fashion, the affirmations of biblical monotheism are

[7] Cf. A. HULSBOCH, "L'attente du salut d'après l'Ancien Testament," in *Irénikon*, 1954, pp. 4–20; G. PIDOUX, "Un aspect négligé de la justice dans l'Ancien Testament, son aspect cosmique," in *Rev. théol. phil.*, 1954, pp. 283–288. Texts are abundant. There is also the theme, as André Neher emphasizes, of the inclusion of the Noachic covenant in the covenant of grace.

[8] Let us refer solely to those in which Ex 3:14 is adopted by Christ (Jn 8:24, 58, and the "I am . . ." passages; Mt 28:20) or is used in reference to Christ (Rev 1:4). Cf. E. STAUFFER, article "Ego," and F. BUECHSEL,

transferred to Jesus Christ. The title *"Kyrios"* very well can be a royal title which does not of itself imply divinity.[9] As applied to Jesus in the apostolic writings and in the faith of the Church, it assimilates Him to the Father at whose right hand He sits enthroned in heaven. Everything which we shall say further on will be an illustration of this. It is most interesting to draw out of these affirmations of faith their theological significance. Let us begin.

From the moment that God was hypostatically united to an individual human nature (*homo Christus Jesus,* 1 Tim 2:5), He was no longer God-for-the-world, He no longer exercised His sovereignty from and through His divine nature alone, but was so and did so from and through the humanity to which He was united in His Person, a humanity which He "assumed for Himself." (We are speaking here of the effect of the design of God as it is realized in time, but if we consider this design in God Himself, it, like God, is eternal: from all eternity, God sees the Word as *incarnandum;* He predestines us in Him, Eph 1:4; He sees the world as saved in Him.) Scholastic theology, adopting certain categories from St. John Damascene, speaks with precision and felicity of the humanity of Christ as a conjoined and living instrument. *Instrument.* This is to say that a cause is elevated and employed by a superior effective force to a higher order of activity: thus, using a number of horse hairs striking a sheep-gut, a violinist draws forth one of the most sublime beauties on earth. . . . *Conjoined.* This is to say that it is united to the superior effective force, in the order of existence and life, as the arm to the violinist, and not simply as the bow to

---

article "Eimi," in *TWNT,* vol. II, pp. 343f., 396f., and Ed. SCHWEIZER, *Ego Eimi. Die religionsgeschtl. Herkunft und theolog. Bedeutung der johanneischen Bildreden,* Göttingen, 1939. G. GLOEGE says (*Reich Gottes u. Kirche im N.T.,* Gütersloh, 1929, pp. 109–110): "*In seinem Handeln* (= *Christi*) *ist Gottes Handeln in seiner königlichen Fülle Gegenwart geworden.*"

[9] Cf. L. CERFAUX's articles, beginning in 1922, reprinted in *Recueil . . . ,* vol. I.

the arm. *Living.* This is to say that the instrument here is not solely a physical organ, but a being who is conscious, thinking, loving and willing. To say that the Lordship of God is communicated to Jesus Christ means that it dwells in His consciousness, His understanding, His heart and will of man, and that every exercise of this Lordship involves an act of knowledge, love and will on the part of the Holy Servant and Child of God, Jesus Christ. It is not unusual that the service of Christ the King is so often connected, in the Catholic mind, to the worship of the Sacred Heart, since the theological basis of that worship is nothing other than what we have just pointed out. In scholastic theology, one of whose most beautiful chapters is the one *De Christo,* the kingship of Christ is explicitly attributed to His humanity, as one of the consequences of the capital grace (*gratia capitis*) called forth by the grace of union. And, of course, Pauline texts are abundantly cited in this treatment.[10]

From what has preceded, we can readily see that the "economy" has its foundation in "theology." What follows will develop in more detail the bonds which exist between the two. It will also show that if, in the Christ of the incarnation, there is a passage from "theology" to "economy," there will as well finally be a kind of re-absorption of "economy" in "theology."

We would express this economy of the kingship of Christ in the following three propositions. It is a great joy to be able to think that general agreement on them exists among Christians of different Communions.

1. The Lordship of Christ is total and absolute;

2. its full effective exercise is eschatological. Its term is the realization of perfect monotheism.

3. Its "economic" exercise (the earthly administration of the redemption) includes a duality of domains, Church and world, a

---

[10] See St. THOMAS AQUINAS, *Com. in I Cor.,* c. 15, lect. 3; *Sum. theol.,* IIIa, q. 59, a. 2; *Compend. Theol.,* I, c. 241; HUGON and HÉRIS, cited in note 1; J. LECLERCQ, cited *ibid.;* E. MERSCH, *The Whole Christ;* etc.

172

struggle (the resistance of the Powers and of the flesh), and, in Christ Himself, a priestly mode of suffering Servant.

1. The lordship of Christ is total and absolute

This is true *as to its extent or its domain.* One of the most striking characteristics of the affirmations of the New Testament on the lordship of Christ is that this Lordship extends to everything: earthly realities and heavenly realities, the visible and the invisible (Col 1:16; Eph 1:10, 21), the dead and the living (Rom 14:9)—observe the biblical way of expressing totality—"everything" (*ta panta:* cf., *infra,* pp. 136ff.). Christ is *Pantocrator:* Rev 1:8; 4:8; 19:6. Of this "everything," Christ is *the Principle:* Principle of creation (Rev 3:14), of revelation (Jn 8:25; Heb 1:1–4), of redemption (Col 1:18), of resurrection (1 Cor 15:20); He is *the Head:* of all mankind (1 Cor 11:3), of the Church (Col 1:18; 2:10 and 19; Eph 1:22; 4:15; 5:5), of every principle and every power (Col 2:20; compare Eph 1:20f.; 1 Pet 3:22). In Him every right must be "re-headed," taken up under a new Leader (Eph 1:10).

The foundation given by the New Testament to this lordship of Christ corresponds to His domain which is both double and unique, absolutely universal. The New Testament, in fact, links the lordship of Christ sometimes to His position as Son of God (we would say: to the hypostatic union), sometimes to the incarnation and its supreme redeeming moment, the Pasch, which embraces indissolubly the obedience of the cross, the resurrection, the ascension, and the sitting at the right hand of God. It does this most often of all:[11] Rom 1:4; 1 Cor 15:23–28; com-

---

[11] This theme, restored to theological discussion by G. AULEN (*Christus Victor,* New York, 1931; compare R. LEIVESTAD, *Christ the Conqueror,* New York, 1954), was present especially in triumphal Christian art beginning with the fourth century and in the iconography of the cross. Cf. G. GAGE, "La théologie de la victoire impériale," in *Rev. histor.,* 171 (1933), pp. 25f.; "Stauros nikopoios, La victoire impériale dans l'Empire chrétien," in *Rev. Hist. Philos. relig.,* 1933, pp. 370–400.

pare Eph 1:20; Phil 2:6–11 (*dio*); compare Mt 18:18; Heb 4:6f.; Rev 5:9–10, 12 (the Lamb); 19:16. But the lordship of Christ is also connected with the divine filiation of the Son of man: Heb 1:1–4 (heir to all because Son), compare 5:5 as to the priesthood; Jn 1:3–4; 3:35; 5:21; implicitly in Mk 12:35–37; compare the anticipation in Ps 2:7f.; 89:27f. Often, the texts of the New Testament unite the two titles of Creator and Redeemer, by passing from one to the other: 1 Cor 8:6; Col 1:15–20; Heb 1:2–3. The encyclical *Quas primas* of December 11, 1925, which established the yearly feast of Christ the King unites the right of divine sonship and the right of conquest by the cross.[12]

These titles confer on Christ a lordship which can indeed be participated, but which, in its proper dignity, is incommunicable. The name "*Kyrios,*" as belonging to Jesus, is above every name (Phil 2:9; Eph 1:21f.). Among creatures, Christ alone is seated at the right hand of the Father, and thus is the beneficiary of His royal power: Mt 22:44; 26:64; Mk 12:36; 14:62; 16:19; Lk 20:42–43; 22:69; Acts 2:33–36; 5:31; 7:55; Rom 8:34; Col 3:1; Eph 1:20–22; Heb 8:1; 10:12; 1 Pet 3:22; Rev 3:21.

The Old Testament had long since connected the reign of Yahweh in history to His position as Creator. The Psalms frequently pass from the consideration of the cosmic sovereignty of God to the order of salvation and to the praise of His people (see Pss 19; 24; 93; and compare the prayer of Mordecai, Esther 11:8f.). The Messiah had also been foretold in the Old Testament as the one who would accomplish the design of God not only over His people but over His creation as well (cf., for example, Hos 2:23; Is 11; Ps 72:7–12; Dan 7:13–14; and *supra,* note 7). Deliverance or ransom had been described as connected with the power of the Creator and as involving a new creation (Is 43:1f.; 44:24–28; 51:16; 65:17). Christ effectively brings about the design of God in regard not only to His

[12] *AAS,* 17 (1925), pp. 598–599.

people but also to all creation: through Him, the plan of God for man and for the entire world is effected, so that, irrespective of all theological debate (Scotism), it simply must be said that God, in creating the world, really saw it already in Christ.[13] The redemption, the work of His Pasch, sustains not only the covenant but also God's plan for the world, in spite of sin and within the conditions introduced by sin. It is the act through which God, thanks to the obedience of Jesus Christ, puts back into the world the dynamism which will enable His creation to arrive at the end first willed, in spite of sin and the conditions of sin. This is why creative wisdom becomes the wisdom of the cross (see *infra*, 2). This creative wisdom is evidently identical to the eternal Word. But, prior to St. John's demonstration of the identity of the paschal lamb and the Word by which the world was made,[14] St. Paul had broadly applied the themes of wisdom to Christ.[15] He did this precisely to show that the plan of God for mankind and for *the whole of creation* is realized *in and through Christ* who, as Wisdom, and on the basis both of His position as Son (incarnation) and of the obedience of the redeeming cross, contains all (God has filled Him with everything, Eph 1:23), disposes all, leads all to its end.

In our eyes, this is all extremely important. The order of redemption or of grace, on the one hand, and the order of nature or of creation, on the other, have a like basis and spring from a like sovereignty, a like government—those of Jesus Christ,

[13] Cf. 1 Cor 8:6; Col 1:12–20; Eph 1:10 ("recapitulation" theme); Heb 1:1–3 (*plērōma* theme: God fills Christ with everything, and thus "everything" is "filled." Cf. also B. F. WESTCOTT, *Christus Consummator*, London, 1886.

[14] Even in the Old Testament (Sir 9:1f.), then, explicitly, in St. John (1:2–3, 14f.; Rev 19–13), in 2 Pet 3:4–7 and Heb 1:3 (*rēma . . .*), in St. Paul as far as the thought (1 Cor 4:4 and 6; Col 1:15, 17), though not the vocabulary, is concerned, Jesus Christ, the Word, is not only salvific coming and message, but also the creative Word of all things.

[15] Cf. W. S. BOYCOTT, cited *infra*, note 23; A. FEUILLET, "L'Eglise plérôme du Christ, d'après Eph 1, 23," in *NRT,* 76 (1956), pp. 449–472, 593–610.

both as Word or creative Wisdom, and as Word-made-flesh, suffering Servant, and Lamb of God: the Son of man. This unity of source does not entail a unity of structure. In point of fact, Catholic theology distinguishes between "nature" and "grace" to such an extent that an orthodox theologian unjustly reproaches us with having separated them. But it does unquestionably entail a unity of plan and of finality. This means that on the Christological basis of the lordship of Jesus Christ, itself inseparable from the *theology* of the Word,[16] the restoration or re-formation[17] of nature is included in the redemptive plan and in the redemptive power of Jesus Christ. This, once again, implies and signifies that an agreement is in itself possible, that a certain reciprocal ordering and a certain proportion exist between nature and grace, creational order and order of redemption, civilization and evangelization.[18] Our theology of the relationship between nature and grace, our positions on the analogy of being and natural law, are founded on the profound identity and the reciprocal implications of the two aspects of the lordship of Christ.

We are inclined to think that serious misunderstandings exist

[16] J. DANIÉLOU (*The Lord of History*, Chicago, 1958, pp. 183f.) and Charles JOURNET (*The Primacy of Peter. From the Protestant and from the Catholic Point of View*, Westminster, 1954, p. 34) have effectively demonstrated that Jesus, on the level of redemptive *economy*, can realize the design of God on the world only because He *is* the Son of God, the Man-God, the Word incarnate.

[17] This word suggests the Augustinian and medieval schema which classified all God's work according to *Conditio* (creation), *Reformatio* (reshaping redemption), *Consummatio* (eschatology). Compare Th. MICHELIS, cited *supra*, note 1.

[18] When we say "in itself possible," we are not saying that this agreement is obtained by nature independently of God (this would be meaningless), or even independently of Christ. What we mean is that this agreement is bestowed on nature by the Lord as creative Wisdom; that, though affected by sin, it is nevertheless not destroyed, and that Christ, as Redeemer, restores it, gives to it its true end and the possibility of attaining it, but does *not* *create* it. A popularized comparison: suppose a "Sputnik" or "Pioneer" which was, or was not, placed in orbit, which had, or did not have, the power needed to reach its objective.

on these questions between the Reform and ourselves. It is true that the primacy which has been given in scholastic theology to a sapiential if not philosophical approach to things has led to an interest in the *things* themselves, in themselves, and thus to their ontological conditioning rather than their existential relationship in Jesus Christ, the center of the whole economy. The development of the treatise *De Gratia* took place, moreover, in the West, within a tradition which was anthropological and moral above all (St. Augustine against Pelagius; the debates of the sixteenth century with the Reform, those of the seventeenth century among different theological schools or with Jansenism). Much recent discussion or research has shown that, in the Catholic Church, the question of "nature"-and-"grace" still presents problems. . . . The Eastern tradition, whose theology is fundamentally one of the divinization of man and of creation, certainly distinguishes between the two orders, nature and grace,[19] but posits a closer relationship between nature, including cosmic nature, called to be transfigured, and grace. Or, again, between natural knowledge and "pneumatic" knowledge, between nation, or state, and Church. In the West, too, the liturgy, "the great teacher of the Church" (Pius XI), has never ceased to embrace creation within the redemption, and has taken pains to put the life and the world of men under the control of what was done by Christ for us, particularly in His Pasch.[20] But if the order of salvation or of grace is, in the strictest sense, a new creation, calling for a

[19] See G. W. LAMPE, "Some Notes on the significance of Basileia tou Theou, Basileia Christou in the Greek Fathers," in *JTS*, 49 (1948), pp. 58–73.

[20] The early anaphoras give thanks both for the benefits of creation and for those of redemption (of salvation history); the *Roman Martyrology* speaks, at Christmas, of *Consecratio Mundi;* the litanies of the saints ask for the removal of even cosmic evils, in the name of all the events of a thoroughly Christological salvation history; in virtue of the cross, there are blessings and consecrations for earthly realities, and a sacrament, that of marriage, makes holy a natural reality by bestowing upon it a meaning in relationship to Christ and to the Church, etc.

177

new birth,[21] the creational order has nonetheless its own existence, its own goodness and, along with them, a fundamental
aptitude to return to God once a way is opened and given to it by
the eternal Wisdom through whom all things subsist. The insistence on justification by faith alone, the desire to substitute for
scholastic ontology a dramatic and existential view of the religious rapport as one of faith and salvation, and the focaliza-
tion, ultimately, of everything on the Word, have, it seems to us,
led Protestantism to a certain forgetfulness of the cosmic value
of the redemption and of the kingship of Jesus Christ, even
antecedent to eschatology.[22] We are delighted that this value is
today once again recognized in communions stemming from
the Reform.[23]

[21] Cf. 2 Cor 5:17; Eph 2:10; Gal 6:15; Jn 3:3f.; etc.
[22] The observation has been made by a good number of non-Catholic
theologians: H. P. OWEN, cited *infra*, note 23; W. A. VISSER 'T HOOFT, *The
Kingship of Christ*, New York, 1948, pp. 15f.; A. KOEBERLE, in *Theologie
als Glaubenswagnis, Festschrift für K. Heim*, Tübingen, 1954. And cf. following note.
[23] Some references: Anglicans: W. S. BOYCOTT, "Creation and Christology," in *Theology*, 52 (1949), pp. 443–448; "Creation and the Church,"
in *ibid.*, 53 (1950), pp. 455–460; H. P. OWEN, "Creation and Incarnation,
Some further Thoughts," in *ibid.*, 54 (1951), pp. 411–416; L. S. THORN-
TON, *Revelation and the Modern World (The Form of the Servant)*, 2 vols.,
Westminster, 1950f.; *The Dominion of Christ*, Westminster, 1952; J.
MARSH, *The Fullness of Time*, ch. V, London, 1952; A. D. GALLOWAY, *The
Cosmic Christ*, London, 1951. —Congregationalist: C. H. DODD, *Gospel and
Law*, New York, 1951. Lutherans: J. JEREMIAS, *Jesus als Weltvollender*,
Gütersloh, 1930; M. GOGUEL, "Le caractère et le rôle de l'élément cosmo-
logique dans la sotériologie paulinienne," in *Rev. Hist. Philos. rel.*, 15
(1935), pp. 335–359; W. STAEHLIN, "Das Heil der Welt," in *Schriften d.
Theol. Konvents Augsburg. Bekenntnisses*, n. 3, Berlin-Spandau, 1951, pp.
5–26; G. WEHRUNG, *Welt und Reich*, Stuttgart, 1952; J. A. SITTLER, *Called
to Unity*, a report made to the Congress of the World Council of Churches
at New Delhi, published in *Ecumenical Review*, January, 1962, pp. 177–
187: it is a remarkable text, which has provoked considerable discussion
(cf. *Istina*, 1963, p. 374). —Calvinist: W. A. VISSER 'T HOOFT, cited in the
preceding note, and "Redécouverte de l'universalisme christocentrique dans
le mouvement oecuménique," in *Verbum caro*, n. 66, 1963, pp. 214–221.
And see also J.-Ph. RAMSEYER, "Signification de la création," in *Verbum
caro*, 6 (1952), pp. 97–107.

2. The full effective exercise of the lordship of Christ is eschatological. Its term is the realization of perfect monotheism

Christ reigns in heaven. He also reigns on earth, but according to an economy whose different stages must be clearly noted. The *full* effective exercise of the power of Christ,[24] to which *all things* are rightfully subject, would have as its effect the Kingdom. The Kingdom, considered in the light of what it means for creatures, is characterized by two principal features.

a) It will put an end to the situation to which creatures have been doomed because of the revolt of men and a certain domination of the "Powers" (cf. *infra*), and which St. Paul calls "subjection to futility" (Rom 8:20). What this has meant for them is two great evils or rather two great families of evils: 1) the wounding, the degradation, not only of the image and likeness of God but also of the integrity of their powers: for them, sickness, ignorance, suffering, evils of all sorts, are but the advance guard of their ultimate enemy, death. —2) The world is a broken world. Division and opposition exist among beings whose desire is for harmony and communion. Nature is hostile to man; men do not understand one another, but are divided at the very heart of their intimacy; they are divided within themselves. Devotion to the external, often even open hostility and war, and the oppression of the weakest which follows upon them—such is the world's condition.

The Kingdom will be the healing of wounds, the reintegration of diminished beings, the reconfiguration of the distorted Likeness, victory over illness,[25] over ignorance and, finally, over death (1 Cor 15:26, 54). It will also be reconciliation, peace, com-

---

[24] In the Latin of the scholastics: *"executio potestatis."* Thus, St. THOMAS AQUINAS, *Sum. theol.*, IIIa, q. 59, a. 4, ad 2.

[25] This is the significance of many of the miracles in the Gospels, as signs of the approach of the Kingdom of God.

179

munion, the conquest or suppression of the exteriorities and oppositions in which we struggle among ourselves.

b) As the fruit of the full effective exercise of the lordship of Christ, the Kingdom must unite the two realities, now separated, of Church and world, the creational order and the order of the redemption. It will, in fact, be inaugurated by the glorious Parousia of the Lord, which will be like the extension to the World of the reality of His resurrection. What can this mean, if not the ascendancy of the Spirit over creational realities themselves? What can it mean, if not the realization of the glory of God, the true establishment of His reign? Oh, how great is our need for the Lord to return to save everything, to wipe away every tear (Rev 21:4). *Marana tha!* Come, Lord! prays the Church (1 Cor 16:22; Rev 22:17, 20; *Didache* 10:5–6).

Eschatological, parousiacal reign—in the sense of Parousia intended by St. Paul: the final and glorious return of the Lord, analogous to the triumphal entry of a sovereign into one of his cities. This eschatological consummation will not be simply the manifestation of what already exists *in mysterio* (Heb 1:8; Col 3:3–4; 1 Jn 3:2). It involves new acts of the kingly power of Christ; precisely, the exercise of this *power,* not only for the resurrection of the body, for the transfiguration of the world, but also, under its coercive form, for the subjection to Himself, in strict justice, of those who may have resisted the appeal of mercy.

The reign and thus the Kingdom will be perfect only when "God will be everything to everyone" (1 Cor 15:28). St. Paul links this immensely profound declaration of "God everything in every one" to a new and final stage, that of "the end, when he [Christ] delivers the kingdom to God the Father after destroying every rule and every authority and power" (1 Cor 15:24). The reign of God involves two phases. In a first, earthly, phase, its realization is achieved *in Christo,* "in the Lord," but in

180

the Lord precisely as He came to us, namely, *in forma servi* (cf. *infra*, 3). In the final phase, the reign must be that of the Lord *in forma Dei*. Christ Himself will gather the fruits of the victory which He has won for our benefit; He will dry the tears, He will destroy the last enemy, death, He will subdue the Powers which militate against God's being truly and fully God for His creatures. And, having subjected all things to Himself, He will hand the Kingdom over to God the Father, so that God might be everything to every one.

The result of all this will be the perfect realization of full monotheism. This means the total and perfect dependence, joyfully acknowledged, of all things on the one Source of all being, of all truth, of all goodness and of all life. Things, and man who uses them, will cease to style themselves and to will themselves as independent, as the source and the end of their own existence, of their own power; they will then recognize that God is God, they will admit the fact that He is truly God, not only in Himself and for Himself, but in them and for them. This, truly, will be the reign and thus the Kingdom. God will be everything to every one, not by an absurd and impossible pantheism, but by that panentheism spoken of by several religious philosophers.[26] God will do everything in every one. This, truly, will be the sabbath of creation and of history, which the Fathers lyrically named the eighth day (the first of a new world). Yes, a true sabbath, when we shall rest from our labors, when we shall rest from laboring by ourselves, and so receive *everything* from God, with thanksgiving.[27]

[26] There is little doubt that the sophiology of certain Orthodox theologians would have something to tell us on this subject. In the Catholic tradition, there are little more than hints or fragmentary parallels. Even though real, they stem from another climate of thought.

[27] There are wonderful texts from the Fathers which should be read in this connection: ORIGEN, *Comm. in Cant.*, prol. (BAEHRENS edition, p. 84); *In Num. hom.*, XXIII, 4 (p. 216); compare MAXIMUS THE CONFESSOR, *Opusc. ad Marianum* (*PG* 91, 33f.); St. AUGUSTINE, especially, *De Civit. Dei*, XXII, 30, 4–5 (*PL* 41, 803–804); *De Gen. ad litt.*, VI, 25–29 (*PL*

There can be no question of our duty to acknowledge the economic, provisional character of the reign of Christ as Christ, as the envoy of God and the suffering Servant. His royal priesthood is a path to the throne of God and still possesses an intermediary character (Heb 10:20, etc.). The Kingdom, in its earthly and preparatory form, is the Kingdom *of Christ;* in its final perfect form, it will be the Kingdom *of God,* that is, of the Father, of the Source without source: perfect monotheism.[28] In somewhat similar fashion, there had been, in Israel, a return to the lordship of the one Yahweh through the "parenthesis" of the Davidic kingship. . . . The humanity of Jesus is, however, associated[29] with this reign *of God* forever, and all those who have voluntarily subjected themselves to Him will be associated with Him in it (Rev 3:21, and *passim;* Eph 2:6; 2 Tim 2:12).[30]

34, 306–307). Compare what a completely contemporary author has written: "All our questions, all our anxieties, all our grievances spring from the same cause: God is not God for us. . . . Heaven will be to see how God is God" (L. EVELY, *We Dare to Say Our Father,* New York, 1965, p. 8).

[28] There is 1 Cor 15:24–25. But there is also 1 Cor 11:3, "the head of Christ is God"; there are Mt 13:41 (messianic reign) and 43 (Kingdom of the Father), 25:34 (the King, Christ, says: "Come, O blessed *of my Father*"), etc. Jesus organizes the Kingdom, but it is the Father who determines its date: Mt 24:36; Acts 1:7 (Dan 2:21). Note how, in the New Testament, *God* almost everywhere means the Father (cf. Karl RAHNER, "Theos in the New Testament," in *Theological Investigations,* vol. I, Baltimore, 1961, pp. 79–148). It goes without saying that, if the Father is the Principle, the Son and the Holy Spirit are inseparable from Him in perfect monotheism.

[29] Cf. Ps 110 and its utilization in the apostolic kerygma; Dan 1:14; Rev 1:6, and *passim.* On the theme of the Temple, compare Rev 21:22. The idea of a kingship of Christ which is purely economic and transitory was held by Marcellus of Ancyra and condemned.

[30] The Virgin Mary represents a privileged instance of this eschatological spiritual kingship of Christians. The basis of this privileged position is her vocation to be the Mother of God, a vocation which is followed up by a super-eminent degree of grace and spiritual perfection, which places Mary above all men, above the angels, above all other creatures which are creatures alone. But this royalty of Mary remains: 1) a participation in that of Christ; 2) of the same order as that of the Church and of Christians. It is not a sovereign lordship, as Christ's is: He alone is seated "at the right hand *of God*."

182

But in reigning with Him, we will not be "Lord with Him": His *Kyriotēs* will always remain incommunicable.

3. *The "economic" exercise (the earthly administration of the redemption) of His lordship by Christ includes a duality of domains, Church and world, a struggle (the resistance of the Powers and of the flesh), and, in Christ Himself, a priestly mode of suffering Servant*

a) The Lordship which the Father has given to Christ is total: it constitutes Him as Principle and Leader of the world as well as of the Church. We shall not find the distinction between the two in the kingship of Christ, but in the understanding of that kingship which we may or may not possess. The Church is the sphere of Christ's domain where his lordship is recognized and obeyed, where, in other words, He reigns. The World is the sphere where this lordship is ignored or opposed. Thus the lordship of Christ is broader than the sphere in which He reigns and thus is broader than His Kingdom. Even in the eschatological order, Christ will have lordship over hell (cf. Phil 2:10; Rev 5:13), but He will not reign there, except through His power of executing the judgments of His justice. On earth, however, this difference does not solely depend on men. Christ Himself, in obedience to the plan of His Father, did not will to exercise His kingship by exerting a power which He could have imposed with the clearness and compulsion of authority.[31] God respects created freedoms, whose field of exercise is History. He does not use His full power except in occasional fashion, using it to produce "signs" and anticipations, as it were, of the Kingdom which is to come (miracles). His kingship, as it is exercised by Him in

[31] He is King, not of power, but of truth (Jn 18:36–37). Jesus refuses to be proclaimed king (Jn 6:15), He avoids the ambiguity of the messianic title of "Son of David," He forbids the demon to proclaim His character of Christ (Mt 17:1–9; Lk 4:41); He refuses to decide questions of inheritance, etc.

183

the economy of human history, is more or less veiled, weakened and "kenotized" by His mission as suffering Servant and Saviour by the cross. Jesus preferred to call Himself "Son of man." He included under this title two ideas: that of a *celestial* being invested with total lordship (Dan 7:13–14)[32] and that of the suffering Servant of Isaiah. Creative and kingly Wisdom is, here below, the wisdom of the cross, simply because the plan of God is to enter into the conditions of sin and the painful consequences of sin, so as to bring forth victory from them. It is the plan of salvation by the cross, of life coming out of death[33] (and wisdom consists in participating in the plan of God, who *is* Wisdom . . .).

We are all conscious of the ambivalence of the New Testament notion of "world" (cf. Sasse, in *TWNT,* III, pp. 887f., etc.). We think that there are three acceptations of it which can be distinguished:

—created reality in itself, creation (*die Schöpfung*);

—creatures in rebellion against God. Whether the New Testament says "*this* world" to designate the existential world as it is *in concreto,* after the fall, under the sign of evil (*ho kosmos outos = ho aiôn outos:* cf. Rom 12:2; 1 Cor 1:20; 2:6, 12; 3:18f.; 7:31; 10:11; Gal 1:4; 6:14)—or simply says "the world," in the biblical or religious sense, it is the world of men which is meant. (Cf., also, *infra,* regarding the Powers.)

To the extent that "this world" lies under the redemption of Christ, then as to its relationship to Christ and to eschatological salvation, the New Testament freely says "everything" (*ta*) *panta:* Rom 11:36; 1 Cor 11:12; 15:27f.; 2 Cor 6:18; Eph 1:10f., 23; 3:9; 4:10, 15; Col 1:6f., 20; Phil 3:21; compare 1 Tim 6:13; Heb 1:3; 2:8; Jn 1:3; Rev 4:11. All Christian optimism, a Christological optimism, is linked to this accepta-

[32] Cf. A. FEUILLET, "L'Exousia du Fils de l'homme (d'après Mc 2, 10–28 et par.)," in *RechScRel,* 42 (1954), pp. 161–192.

[33] Cf. Lk 24:25f.; Phil 2:6–11; Col 3:4; Heb 2:9; 1 Pet 5:1; compare Ps 110:7, etc. As the Word is the word of the cross (1 Cor 1:18).

tion, which again brings together, in Christ, the primary sense of the word "world" and the initial optimism of Genesis.

b) Christ, our Leader, is enthroned in heaven, at the right hand of the Father. He reigns here below in the Church, but His kingship is still disputed on earth, "until God has put his enemies under his feet."[34] The earthly Kingdom of Christ is still "occupied" by the enemy. The Church is, as it were, "the underground," obeying the orders of the rightful Sovereign who sits afar off, in the heavenly Jerusalem, the *free* Jerusalem, obeying His orders in difficult and burdensome circumstances. But the world, in the second sense we have pointed out, is in ignorance of the lordship of Christ and more or less seriously resists it.

There is still discussion among exegetes[35] about the precise significance of the "Powers" of which St. Paul speaks. Each text of the Apostle evidently has its proper context, hence its proper orientation: the letter to the Romans (Chapter 13) is aimed at the problems which arose in the capital of the empire; the captivity epistles are aimed at a kind of gnosis and seek to affirm, in opposition to that gnosis, that *even the Powers* are subject to Christ as to the absolute Leader of everything. Agreement can, it seems, be reached on the basis of this rather ample view: the *Dunameis* are forces which are, either both or in the alternative, personal and collective, superior and immanent to the great realities of the world or of history.[36] These forces tend to divert

---

[34] Ps 110:1, so often quoted in the apostolic kerygma: Acts 2:34f.; Mt 22:44; Mk 12:36; Heb 1:13; 8:1; 10:12–13; 12:2; 1 Pet 3:22; compare also Acts 7:55; Rom 8:34; Eph 1:20; Col 3:1, and C. H. DODD, *According to the Scriptures. The Substructure of the New Testament*, London, 1952, pp. 34–35.

[35] Cf. F. KEIENBURG, *Die Geschichte der Auslegung v. Römer 13, 1–7*, Gelsenkirchen, 1952, pp. 128f. Since then there has appeared Heinrich SCHLIER, *Principalities and Powers in the New Testament*, New York, 1961.

[36] Holy scripture presents other cases which are more or less related, and of a like lack of distinctiveness: cf. Rev 13 and 17, the beast, the false prophet, whom Christ must overcome.

creation (Scripture does not here distinguish between nature and men) from the end willed by God, by inciting it to seek the independent accomplishment of their destiny, to live and to act by their own power (*"Eigenmächtigkeit"*) and solely in view of itself. Put very briefly, this is the contrary of full monotheism, which is theonomic. The "Powers" are that which assumes a leader's role, even to the extent of giving a meaning to things and to the life of men, within the exclusive limits of the present world (compare St. John Chrysostom, *Hom. 7 in 1 Cor.,* n. 1). We will see further on (§ c) what this means in the concrete. Here we will do no more than note its kinship with the great idea of St. Augustine, which has been shown by E. Bernheim to have dominated the medieval conception of History: *"quaerere quae sua sunt"*: "Two loves have built two cities . . ." (*De Civit. Dei,* 14, 28; *PL* 41, 436).

Now if Christ has already been victorious over the Powers (1 Pet 3:22), if He has already received the kingship *of the world* (Rev 11:15), it is nonetheless said of Him that he *will* reign (*ibid.*), that He has delivered us, but that He *will* deliver us from death (Rom 8:11), that He has conquered (Jn 16:33; Rev 3:21), and that He *will* conquer (Rev 6:2; 17:14). There has already been a first victory over Satan (Jn 12:31), but there must be a second (Rev 12:10). In brief, Jesus is the Lord of the world, but He must still become its Lord, and He will not be fully proclaimed as such except in His return in power and majesty. The activity of His faithful cooperates in His victory throughout the course of history, by weakening the power of the occupying force and causing the boundaries of its empire to recede (cf. *infra,* § c). And the same is true of the prayer of the saints in heaven.[37]

[37] Cf. Rev 6:9–10; compare Lk 18:7. The prayer of the saints hastens the eschatological era, at the same time as the combat and the missionary activity of the faithful on earth. May it be that the reign of a thousand years, in Rev 20:1–6, is to be identified with the reign of the saints (the

186

c) Thus, when we affirm the kingship of Christ over the world, His truly cosmic lordship, we realize that here below this kingship is not a domination of power (Mt 26:53; Jn 18:36); Jesus Himself was very careful to put a distance between His authority and all power of a temporal type (cf. Mk 10:42f.; Lk 22:25f.; Jn 13:12f.). His is the kingship of the suffering Servant, a kingship of a prophet-king (cf. Jn 18:37) and victim. It is a pleasure to quote here the very lovely phrase from *Le Songe du Vergier* (fourteenth century) which says that Christ was not *"seigneur seigneurisant en la temporalité"* ("a lord lording it over the things of the world").

The kingship of Christ is priestly and prophetic, just as His priesthood is prophetic and kingly, and His quality of prophet kingly and priestly. The three functions of Christ, among which there exists a kind of *"perichoresis,"* can no more be separated than one can dissociate the four marks of the Church, which reciprocally modify one another. Instinctively, we tend to bring about the perfect coincidence of holiness, knowledge, and power (the three orders of Pascal, briefly stated; *Pensées,* no. 793). In point of fact, they were made to coincide but, here below, they do not always do so: power is sometimes ignorant and malign, holiness is generally deprived of power. Besides, when he must make a choice among the three, carnal man prefers power, wealth: Adam sacrificed the obedience of faith for his own independence. Christ sacrifices kingly prestige for filial submission. He appears "in His order of holiness." In its *forma servi,* the reign of Christ is less imperial than prophetic and priestly. His lordship, which by right is universal and cosmic, is principally and directly exercised in the spiritual and religious order;[38] in the domain of consciences, of human freedom (cf. Jn 18:37),

---

martyrs), with Christ in heaven during the era of the Church? However that may be, the Holy Office has decreed that mitigated millenarianism *"tuto doceri non potest"* (Decree of July 20th, 1944, *AAS,* 36 (1944), p. 212).

[38] Compare PIUS XI, encyclical *Quas primas, AAS,* 17 (1925), p. 600.

and, with certain exceptions, in the political or physical domain, it is exercised only through men, by means of their interior transformation. Here below, Jesus transforms the World by converting and by sanctifying souls.

We have here, for example, one meaning of passages like Mt 9:1–8; Mk 2:1–11, where Jesus says to the paralytic who expects to be healed by Him: "Your sins are forgiven." We have one meaning for the choice by the Latin liturgy of Jn 20:19–23 for the Gospel of the Votive Mass for Peace: peace based on forgiveness of sins and interior conversion by the Holy Spirit. Jesus acts especially in this world as Saviour, and through the means of salvation. The *exousia* (cf. *supra,* note 32) which He exercises therein is primarily that by which He pardons sin and heals sinners. Was it not in this very sense that Pius XI said that the Church does not evangelize by civilizing, but civilizes by evangelizing?[39]

Further, although Christ is truly Lord of the world, He exercises His kingship, during the interval which separates His coming in humility from His coming in glory, principally over *men.* He reigns in the hearts of men. For us and for the Church, what "bringing about the kingship of Christ" especially means is making God reign *in the human use we make of the world,* in the value we attribute to it. It is, then, wholly appropriate that revelation speaks to us principally of the spiritual rapport we must realize with God, based on faith, and of the *meaning* which our life in the world has from the standpoint of this rapport.

The condition of the disciples follows that of the Master (Mt 10:24; Lk 6:40). Faith, the baptismal consecration, the celebration of the Eucharist place them in the Kingdom of Christ (Col 1:13) and make of them a royal priesthood (1 Pet 2:9). We shall reign with the glorified Christ in a reign of glory and

[39] *Ad sensum* in the letter of Cardinal PACELLI, Secretary of State, to the *Semaine sociale de Versailles,* July 10th, 1936.

even of power.[40] We shall judge even the angels (1 Cor 6:2–3). Even in this reign of glory, we shall sing to the lordship of Christ the praise which belongs only to Him. But we shall be glorified with Him only if we are associated with Him in His suffering, in His humble service of love, only if we accept the humbling conditions of faith, where there are more questions, more difficulties than solutions, and the conditions of love, which bestows more benefits than it receives, and especially than it expects. Here below, the kingship of the Christian over the world is spiritual most of all: it consists most of all in serving the world in love, as created by God, as made for God, and in despising the world, occasionally even in leaving it, as perverse or equivocal.

2. The Lordship of Christ over the Church

Without attempting to define here the theses of an ecclesiology, or even to proceed on the somewhat prejudiced basis of an ecclesiological synthesis, we shall successively envisage the Church as ministry and the Church as faithful people: *Ecclesia congregans* and *Ecclesia congregata* (*in Christo*). It should be understood that these are not two Churches, but two aspects of one same Church.

Because Christ the Lord is master of time, and because His is a royal power, He effectively exercises His prophetic office and His priestly office *in time*. The crucial text in this regard is the one from the last part of Matthew (28:18–20): "'All authority in heaven and on earth has been given to me. GO THEREFORE and make disciples of all nations, baptizing them in the name of the Father and of the Son and of the Holy Spirit, teaching them to observe all that I have commanded you; and lo, I am with you always, to the close of the age.'" Jesus explicitly establishes the

[40] Cf. Dan 7:18, 22, 27; Mt 25:34; compare Lk 12:32; 22:29; Rom 5:17; I Thess 2:12; Eph 2:6; Rev 3:2; 5:10; 20:6; 22:5. And compare *supra,* note 31.

189

triple ministry—prophetic, priestly and royal—of the apostles, and the salvific efficacy of this ministry,[41] on the sovereignty of His kingly power. If the ministries of the Church can be of value for eternal life, the reason is that the Lordship of Christ dominates both heaven and earth.

The ministries instituted and passed down to the apostles are not the only ones which build up the Church. There is a very great variety of gifts which are bestowed in view of general usefulness: the lists given by St. Paul are not exhaustive. It is *the Lord* who distributes them (1 Cor 12:4), exactly as He gives to each his measure of faith (1 Cor 3:5). It is His authority as *Kyrios* that the apostles invoke when they themselves authoritatively act in the matter of teaching or of pastoral government.[42] It is the authority of the *Kyrios* which is the foundation for that of the ministerial acts.

In line with what we have just said, we would like to recommend one point for consideration by the Study Commission of the World Council of Churches. It would undoubtedly lead to one more bond between the more ecclesiological work of the Faith and Order group and the work, principally Christological and missiological in orientation, of the Council as a whole.

The total lordship of Christ, which is prophetic and priestly as well, forms the foundation of the apostolic powers; it forms the foundation of the sacraments (cf., for example, Jn 3:3–7, with reference to 1:12f.); it forms the foundation of Christian preaching to the extent that it is endowed with force (Rom 1:16; Eph 3:7; etc.) and even in its weakness; it forms the foundation of the solidity of the promises by which the Church lives. One of these promises, in many respects the principal one, is the one which is contained in Mt 16:18–19, and which must not be

[41] Compare Mt 16:19; 18:18 (+ Jn 20:23); and the pericope Mk 1:1–12 (= Mt 9:2–8; Lk 5:17–26), in regard to which see note 32, *supra*.

[42] Cf. 1 Cor 1:10; 5:4; 7:10, 12 and 25; 9:14; 15:23; 1 Thess 4:15; and cf. 2 Cor 10:8; 13:10; the *Kyrios* qualifies the apostles to be ministers of a new covenant: 2 Cor 3:6.

190

separated from 28:18, 20 (and also Jn 1:13). Within this ensemble of ecclesial realities, which it would take too long to give in detail, we see the constitution of the Church as a divine institution which is placed in the world: an institution *of divine right,* whose foundation is neither the flesh, nor the will of man, but the Father Himself in the exercise of His Lordship through and in the Lordship He has given to Christ as His own ("My Father who is in heaven. And I tell you . . .": Mt 16:17–18).[43] The Lordship of Christ is not only exercised in vertical and charismatic fashion, as of course it has been (cf. Gal 1:1, 12; etc.)—our formal ecclesiology (though not the *life* of the Church) perhaps does not sufficiently take account of this!—but it is also exercised within the horizontal of time. Like greatness manifesting itself bodily in history, but not coming from history, like greatness founded on the paschal and eschatological divine right of the Kingdom whose King has placed it on earth, the Church represents in the world the prophetic and priestly kingship of Jesus Christ. Those who accept this kingship in faith also accept the kingship, wholly subordinated but nonetheless real, which the Lord has communicated to His spouse in the form of spiritual authority. Baptism inscribes us in the Kingdom of Jesus Christ, it incorporates us in the splendid army of the "saints" (Col 1:12–14). At the same time, it constitutes us as members of the Church, subject to everything which she represents of the

---

[43] We give here, for its density and suggestive character, the following text from a Catholic jurist: "*In der grossen Geschichte der römischen Kirche steht neben dem Ethos der Gerechtigkeit auch das der eigenen Macht* [. . .]. *Die Kirche will die königliche Braut Christi sein; sie repräsentiert den regierenden, herrschenden, siegenden Christus. Ihr Anspruch auf Ruhm und Ehre beruht im eminenten Sinne auf dem Gedanken der Repräsentation* [. . .]. *Dass sie Christus nicht als einen Privatmann und das Christentum nicht als Privatsache und reine Innerlichkeit auffasst, sondern zu einer sichtbaren Institution gestaltet, das ist der grosse Verrat, den man der römischen Kirche zum Worwurf macht*" (C. SCHMITT, *Römischer Katholizismus und politische Form,* München, 1925, p. 43). In more theological style: J.-P. MICHAEL, "Jesus Christus, Erlöser und Gesetzgeber," in *Wort und Wahrheit,* 8 (1953), pp. 581–591.

prophetic, priestly, and royal authority of Christ. It is hardly surprising that a St. Clement of Rome, a contemporary of the apostles, a St. Ignatius of Antioch, and then Tertullian, St. Cyprian, etc., should have lengthened the New Testament (Johannine especially[44]) schema: God the Father (monotheism) → Jesus Christ → apostles and Church, by putting obedience to deacons, priests and bishops in the very line or path as obedience to Christ and to the Father. Royal monotheism, once it has become Christological, finally acquires an ecclesiological image.

Would this mean that the Church, as spouse and body of Christ, is queen over the world, *as* He Himself is King? If the Second Adam has the Church as the New Eve (a patristic commonplace), would the *Kyrios* have, as associate, a *Kyria?* During the Middle Ages, it occasionally happened that some theologians or canonists pursued this assimilation of the "Church" to Christ, thanks to a completely abstract deductive reasoning process, and actually came up with theses of *Weltherrschaft.* Recent historical studies have shown that this was actually far rarer than had been thought by historians, Protestant especially, at the end of the nineteenth and the beginning of the twentieth century. These studies have especially exonerated Gregory VII and Innocent III.[45] The truth is that the Church has indeed received a communication of the kingship of Christ; her prophetic office and her priesthood are equally royal. But this participation leaves to Christ the transcendence of His kingship, prophetic office and priesthood, and is strictly measured by the positive institution of the Lord, in accordance with the economy planned by the

[44] Jn 17:18; 20:21; compare 4:38 (compare 17:18, 26, love; 10:14–15, knowledge; Rev 3:21; 2:26, 28, glory. And see R. BRECHET, "Du Christ à l'Eglise: Le dynamisme de l'Incarnation dans l'Evangile de saint Jean," in *Divus Thomas* (Piacenza), 56 (1953), pp. 67–98).
Compare Lk 22:29–32; Rom 1:3–6; 1 Cor 3:23; Acts 9:4. Clement, *Corinthians* 4, 1–2; Tertullian, *De Praescr.,* 21, 4.
[45] But not Innocent IV; nor Boniface VIII either, perhaps.

Father. The Church's law is the very one formulated by the Gospel: *"Ministrare, non ministrari,"* but, even without taking into account the impact of historical situations, it is a law which the spirit of the flesh obviously tends always to forget. The kingship thus communicated to the Church is, in the *Ecclesia congregata* or the *Societas fidelium,* essentially spiritual (cf. *supra*); in the *Ecclesia congregans* or apostolic-hierarchical institution, it consists in a *religious* authority, measured by the purposes of salvation and of the spiritual mission of the Church. But, within this order, it is real.

In a society such as ours, which is pervaded by secularist ideas, we must remember that Jesus Christ is an authority, that He has legislated, that He has placed in the world a people and a kingdom whose principle of existence, not only an interior and spiritual principle but a juridical principle, too, is divine. In a society such as ours, which is individualistic to the point of anarchy, we must, without losing sight of the extremely profound theme of Christian freedom, remember the Christian idea of obedience. Obedience is not just a matter of what we have to do for one another, through one another, in view of our common destiny according to the plan of God; obedience effects an important segment of the truth of inter-membral relationships within a differentiated and ordered body (God is not a God of disorder . . . : 1 Cor 14:33). While effecting the interlocking of the members in this body, it also effects an acknowledgment of the lordship of Christ, master of order. Thus, speaking to women, to children, to slaves, but also to the faithful in respect of the leaders of communities, Saint Paul enjoins them to be obedient "in the Lord," just as he asks husbands, masters, superiors, to command "in the Lord."[46] Every Christian encounters Christ in his brothers and in his superiors (even the difficult ones!

---

[46] 1 Cor 7:21–23; Eph 6; Col 3:22f.; Tit 2:9–10; 1 Pet 2:18. In the ecclesial order: Heb 13:17; 1 Cor 16:16; Phil 2:29–30; 1 Thess 5:12–13; 1 Tim 5:17; etc.

1 Pet 2:18) or subordinates, and he is called to realize his life as a life "in the Lord," in this very situation, in these very encounters. It is of course perfectly clear that obedience is not the only virtue of the Christian life, any more than it is the answer to all questions.

The kingship of Christ is not only *in* the Church, communicated partially to the Church, it is also *over* the Church. The New Testament actually expresses the relationship which exists between Christ and the Church along two lines, but it does not separate these lines. The synoptic Gospels show us a Christ whose personal relationships with His disciples was especially one of authority or power. St. John shows Him to us as establishing between Himself and His own a relationship of mystical identity (cf. Chapter 15). These two relationships are united in the notion of spouse, or in the notion of body, of which St. Paul was fond. The Apostle shows, on the one hand, the Church as body of Christ, having a mystical, that is spiritual and secret, identity with Christ, and, on the other hand, Christ as Head or Leader of His body, Lord of the Church.[47]

"And the Lord added to their number day by day those who were being saved" (Acts 2:47). The *Kyrios* Himself directs all the life and growth of His Church. There is no deed of faith or of charity in the world which does not involve an act of knowledge or of will on the part of the Lord Jesus. It is He who converts, either in cooperating sovereignly in the apostolic activity (cf. Mk 16:20, and the case, for example, of Lydia, Acts 16:14), or by preceding the apostolate: the case, for example, of the conversion of Paul, or of Cornelius (Acts 9 and 10), where it is

---

[47] It is very important to observe on this subject that the notion of *kephalē*, in its application to Christ, is not introduced by St. Paul as an elaboration of the comparison of the body, as if Christ were, *in the whole body*, what the head is in our organism. Thematically, it stems from another context and from another concern: the desire to affirm that Christ is *above* the Church, *above* the Powers.

194

noteworthy that, if the Lord acts with a sovereign initiative, He disposes all things in view of an incorporation in the institutional Church.

The Lord also sovereignly leads, in its great lines and its critical moments at least, the historical life of His Church. Instituting the yearly feast of Christ the King in 1925, the year of the sixteenth centenary of the Council of Nicaea, Pius XI saw in that council a victory of Christ the King over heresy.[48] It is in the same sense that Pius XII declared his conviction that his condemnation of atheistic communism would be ratified at the judgment (Christmas Message, 1951). These are only two examples. We could refer to a thousand facts in the life of the Church, in which we could properly see one of the visits, for judgment or for mercy, in which the Lord, outside of His glorious Parousia, returns unceasingly in the Church and in the World.[49] Is it not this for which we are all waiting and praying, in the great ecumenical hope: a parousia, not of judgment but of mercy, which would be eminently a royal act of Christ, if it be true that peace and the unity of a people are the final end of the government of their king.

The apostolate is a *ministry*[50] pure and simple. What St.

[48] Encyclical *Quas primas, AAS*, 17 (1925), pp. 595, 607.

[49] Many passages of the Gospel which apparently antedate the Pauline texts on the Parousia suggest that the return of Christ in His reign begins immediately after He has left this world and has been enthroned on the right hand of God. There is a truth present in the seating and in the subjection of foes (Ps 110:1), and in the coming on the clouds (Dan 7:13; Mk 14:62; etc.), which is coextensive with the time of the Church. See A. FEUILLET, in *RB*, 56 (1949), pp. 72–73; *RechScRel*, 42 (1954), p. 186, and "Le sens du mot Parousie dans l'Evangile de saint Matthieu: Comparaison entre Mat. 24, et Jac. 5, 1–11," in *The Background of the New Testament and its Eschatology . . . in honor of C. H. Dodd*, Cambridge, 1956, pp. 261–280. Compare Fr. SPADAFORA, *Gesù e la fine di Gerusalemme*, Rovigo, 1950. Texts such as Mt 10:23; 16:28; 24:30, 34; 26:64, speak of a return of Christ to do judgment on His people, one which is different from the eschatological return. Amos, Ezekiel (concerning the remnant), Daniel have already acquainted us with such comings.

[50] Cf. 2 Cor 3:6; 11:23; Eph 3:7; Col 1:23.

Thomas Aquinas wrote about the rejection by the Greeks of the primacy of the pope and the *filioque* can be applied to the whole Church, to all that is done in it by the ministries: these two errors, he said, indicate an identical failure of appreciation. "For Christ, the Son of God, consecrates *His* Church for Himself by *His* Holy Spirit, and impresses the mark of the Spirit upon her as a spiritual seal. And, similarly, the vicar of Christ, by the primacy and the charge he exercises, as a faithful minister preserves the universal Church in submission to Christ."[51] As a matter of fact, the Holy Spirit and the ministry have, each in its own order, been predisposed by Christ to do His work. The one works within, the other without, in a harmonious way and in a kind of concelebration.[52] Like the sending of the apostles, the sending of the Holy Spirit is a kingly act,[53] which fills up the interval between Pasch and Parousia, the interval which is the era of the Church, the era of mission. During this interval, the Spirit of Christ and the Church of Christ, both of which proceed, as "sent," from the incarnation and Pasch of the Lord, are active in behalf of the reign of Christ, whose coming in glory they call forth (Rev 22:17).

We can readily see that the carnal spirit—the spirit of power and of will to dominate—has also been active within the Church, among men of the Church. Under the guise of the instinct which leads us to desire the coincidence of holiness and power, such forces have sometimes turned the pure service of the Lordship of Christ into clericalism and "ecclesiocracy." Through the Spirit of Christ, who inspires perpetual "spiritual" renewals

---

[51] *Contra errores Graecorum,* II, 21. *Opera,* Parma edition, vol. XV, p. 256. What is to be emphasized in this text is more the ecclesiological suggestion than the polemical position.

[52] See Y. M.-J. CONGAR, "The Holy Spirit and the Apostolic Body, Continuators of the Work of Christ," pp. 147–186, in *The Mystery of the Church,* Baltimore, 1960.

[53] Cf. Jean BOSC, *L'office royal du Seigneur Jésus-Christ,* Genève, 1957, pp. 85f. (ET *The Kingly Office of the Lord Jesus Christ,* Edinburgh, 1959).

within her, the Church must struggle unceasingly against the carnal within herself and thus remain subject to her Lord.

3. The Exercise of the Lordship of Christ over the World

The lordship of Christ is total. Even so, it allows for the duality, in the present economy, of Church and world. Both are subject to this Lordship, but under different conditions. The Spirit, whose perfect ascendancy will make the Kingdom come, is the proper principle of existence and life in the Church, but not in the World. This is sufficient to make of the Church, beginning here below, the germinal cell of the Kingdom; but, since the Spirit is given only in pledge, it is not sufficient to make of the world temple of God and Church. Consequently, the lordship of Christ is exercised here below according to two irreducible registers which, though normally made to be in harmony, are often enough discordant—within the very structures of the natural world, and by reason of ecclesial structures. These two registers must be considered separately and successively.

1. *The lordship of Christ over the world being exercised within the creational structures of the world*

Our knowledge of the transfer to Christ of the monotheistic affirmations, and our knowledge of the fashion in which St. Paul and St. John spoke of Christ as Wisdom or as the Word by which God created, conserves and governs all things, permit us to maintain the Christological foundation of all the energies of creation, all the powers and authorities of the age.[54] Through

---

[54] The texts of the New Testament on political power are not expressly Christological: Rom 13:1–7; 1 Tim 2:2; Tit 3:1; 1 Pet 2:12f. (where *dia ton Kyrion* undoubtedly refers to the teaching and example of Christ); Jn 18:33–37. Tradition (in the West, following GELASIUS particularly; cf. JAFFE, *Regesta Pontificum Romanorum,* Leipzig, 1885, 632 and 701), the

them, though of course within the limitation of the legitimacy of their power and prescriptions, we obey the Lord. The Catholic Church has consistently preached and practiced loyalty to constituted authority, and respect for things.

a) *This* world not only does not know that Christ is its center of gravity and guides it towards its destiny, but it rejects Jesus Christ (Jn 1:5, 11; 3:11; 10:26) and crucifies the Lord of glory (1 Cor 2:8). The cry of the Jews is the world's cry, and it is our cry, to the extent that we are carnal and belong to it: *Tolle eum!* Take Him away! In the strictest possible sense, sin takes God away from the world, while activity according to true monotheism, activity according to the plan of God, according to grace, makes God come to the world in His lordship. The Gospel according to St. John shows us the trial of Jesus as necessarily continuing throughout history and shows us the role of the Holy Spirit in manifesting the justice of Jesus, so as to demonstrate that the world was wrong in condemning Him, and to console the witnesses of Christ in this gigantic struggle (Jn 16:8–11).[55]

This world has its prince, whom the New Testament refers to under different names.[56] Even though he has already been conquered by Christ,[57] and is being conquered unceasingly by the same Christ in the faithfulness of Christians,[58] he is still "the spirit that is now at work in the sons of disobedience" (Eph 2:2).

---

liturgy (that of consecrations, in particular), art, in the West as well as in the East, finally—in part—medieval theology have often made explicit the Christological basis of the temporal power.

[55] Cf. Théo PREISS, *La justification dans la pensée johannique,* in *Hommage et reconnaissance à Karl Barth,* Paris-Neuchâtel, 1947, pp. 100–118; M. F. BERROUARD, "Le Paraclet, défenseur du Christ devant la conscience du croyant" [Jn 16:8–11], in *Rev. Sc. Phil. theol.,* 33 (1949), pp. 361–389 (Bibliography).

[56] Jn 12:31; 14:30; 16:11; 1 Jn 5:19. —God of this world: 2 Cor 4:4; compare Eph 2:2; 6:12 (the spirit of wickedness, whose abode is between heaven and earth).

[57] Jn 12:31; 16:11 and 33; Eph 1:21; Col 2:15; 1 Pet 3:22; Heb 2:14.
[58] Cf. Col 1:13; 2:20; 1 Jn 2:13–14; 4:4; 5:5, and Rev.

We know that, with their human henchmen, the beast, the false prophet, the Antichrist. . . , the Prince of this World and the Powers turn creation away from following the law of God, from obeying the "consistent monotheism" whose formula, which says all that must be said, is: that God might be God! They incite the creatures of God to the will towards autonomy. But as, in man, where the different psychic or physical energies, instead of accepting their subordination to one another and working harmoniously together, assert their independence, bring about physical or psychic illness, so is the "independent" creature really distorted and sick, no matter what its apparent successes might be. The possessed souls of the Gospels are also sick men, debased men.[59]

It is especially in the world of men that the Powers make their mark. By employing the old line of absolute independence (Gen 3:5), the Prince of this World and his henchmen urge men to replace theonomic attitudes with the pursuit of tempting goals. These are the age-old idols: the lust of the flesh, the lust of the eyes and the pride of life (1 Jn 2:16). The holy victory of Christ in His triple temptation, which could be easily related to this triple concupiscence, is also a basis of His kingship. The demon might well have wished to lead Jesus towards the idea of a messianism of power and prodigy, but Jesus remained obedient to the Father.

Another age-old demon is the quest for self-justification, which can be shown as one of the great moving powers in history.[60] There are, finally, the religious demons, not only those of idolatry, but also those of false images of God, against which the prophets of Israel conducted so difficult a struggle: God downgraded into social or emotional security, into the Ceres of good harvests or the Mercury of favorable winds. . . .

But there are also idols more particularly modern or con-

[59] Cf. Mt 9:2 and 4:24; 8:16; Lk 13:16; Acts 10:38; 1 Jn 3:8.
[60] Herbert BUTTERFIELD, *Christianity and History,* London, 1949.

temporary. These are sometimes things which are good in themselves, but which are given a value which is not according to God: a value of messianism, hence of final salvation (the beast, which certainly seems to be political power seeking to make itself totalitarian and messianic, has itself adored as God: Rev 13). Here is a list, obviously incomplete, of the idols which, along with the age-old idols, seduce the man of today. It is not difficult to see in it the privileged field of action of the Powers, if it be true that the demon is intent upon domination over all those structures in which man encounters a diminution in force of his choices and inclinations): race, class, nation, the cause, the party, progress, humanity, sometimes science, technology and the comforts they produce. Money which, with the spirit of possession, St. Paul refers to as an idolatry (Col 3:5; Eph 5:5). Occasionally, the body, health. And, in the religious field, juridicalism, legalism, which foster a sort of replacement of the end by the means; superstition, ritualistic religion (cf. Gal 4:8–10); finally, certain gnoses or false mysticisms. . . .

b) Defeated and subdued, the Powers will return in the triumph of Christ. Creation, to the extent that it is freed from the equivocal or sinful conditions of *this* world, to the extent that it is simply *ta panta,* must, under Christ as Leader, be brought around to the accomplishment of the plan of God. On the other hand, even through the history of *this world,* the powers of the earthly city do the work of Christ in keeping evil in check (this is one of Christ's functions: 1 Thess 4:6, *ekdikos,* the same word which is used in 1 Pet 2:14) and also in fostering good (cf. note 54). Honor paid to the king is spoken of, in 1 Pet 2:17, as akin to the fear of God. The faithful see God and find His will in all lawful and authentic and natural commands.

Those men who, without knowledge of God in Christ, seek after justice, also give honor to this Lordship, but without knowing it and without doing Him glory; they thereby risk attributing to idols the glory which is due to God alone (cf. Rom 1:18–23). Consequently, men who are strangers to the knowledge of God and of Jesus Christ do the work of their royal will within the structures of Creation, but they do it in the area of ambiguity and are in danger of promoting the *reign* of idols and of sin. And yet, there is something positive in every work of authentic justice, in respect of the Kingdom of God. Healing the sick, knowing and making known the natural truth of things, assuring the reign of human justice, suppressing the various forms of slavery, freeing man, putting at the disposal of others more of the goods of creation: all of these are activities which, to the extent that they are authentic, really accomplish the work of God, even while involving the risks of ambiguity and of openness to the reign of sin, as we have said. In its deepest movement, human history is ultimately a search for the two benefits, healing or wholeness, and unification or universal reconciliation, which the Kingdom will bestow on the creature. The Kingdom, though, will produce them from above, whereas history seeks to obtain them from below, through the resources of the creature itself. To the extent that the effort of men brings into play the authentic energies of creation, and fulfills the program initially given to "multiply, and fill the earth and subdue it" (Gen 1:28), that effort labors for Christ who, eternal Wisdom, embraces the purposes of Creation in the work of its redemption.

We also find in Christian tradition, and even in St. Augustine, the theme of natural blessings and that of natural preparations for the Gospel.[61] Catholic teaching affirms the radical goodness of nature, its proportion or possible harmoniousness, with the free gifts of goodness and justice.[62] The Word, the very Word who

[61] A notion accepted in the encyclical *Evangelii Praecones* of Pius XII, June 2nd, 1951, nos. 58, 62.

[62] This is not an attribution of goodness to the creature independently of the plan of God—this would be idolatry, the negation of full monotheism—but, on the contrary, a way of relating to God, the God of Abraham,

became man, died, rose again, ascended to heaven so as to fill everything (Eph 4:10), would enlighten every man coming into this world (Jn 1:9). We know, of course, to what extent these elements of nature are in fact penetrated by the weaknesses, the ambiguities, the distortions which come from sin. Concretely, there is no natural world, but only a sinful and redeemed world. This is a classic thesis in Catholic theology. But (and this is something we must recognize), it is all too easy (and dangerous!) to turn the legitimate distinction between nature and grace into a separate consideration, and to speak of nature as if it were not the nature of a sinful humanity which is in need of the gracious help of God.

The theme of evangelical preparation can be viewed in a narrower way than that of natural law and the radical goodness of creational structures. It can, that is to say, be viewed simply in the framework of the divine government of the world tending towards the realization of the positive design of grace *in Christo et in Ecclesia*. We can already perceive in the Old Testament the fact that historical preparations exist, that a certain historical conditioning of the facts of salvation history thereby exists as well, and in these facts a providential character can be recognized. If this is true at the biblical level, it is still more true in the historical life of the Church, which is more dependent on human history. This provides a kind of preparation for, or anticipations (partial, to be sure!) of the sovereign act by which Christ, master of time, wills to "re-head" all things, and thus lead the very history of the world to serve His reign. But we must not hide from ourselves the truth that, within the course of history, human factors condition the life of the people of God in a pernicious way, and these factors will fall under the judgment. This is, in particular, the case of the different syncretisms, in Israel and

---

of Isaac, and of Jacob, to the God of Jesus Christ, everything that is good in creation. Compare A. AUER, "Die Fülle der Zeiten," in *Theologisches Denken als Deutung der Zeit,* Salzburg, 1946, pp. 65f.